CHURCH PLANTING WORKBOOK

A GLOBAL PROVEN, PRACTICAL GUIDE TO PLANTING DYNAMIC CHURCHES

DR. HENDRIK J. VORSTER

CHURCH PLANTING WORKBOOK
By Dr. Hendrik J. Vorster
A practical guide to Planting Dynamic Churches
This Handbook explores parts of the content contained in: "Church Planting - How to plant a dynamic Church"
as well as in
"Values of the Kingdom of God," and
"Spiritual disciplines of the Kingdom of God."

Apart from this Handbook, you will also need the following items to complete your study:

1. A Good Version of the Bible.
2. A pen or pencil to write the answers.
3. Coloured pencils (red, blue, green and yellow).

www.churchplantinginstitute.com
resources@churchplantinginstitute.com
Or
www.churchplantingdoctor.com
resources@churchplantingdoctor.com

Copyright © churchplantingdoctor.com All rights reserved.
No part of this publication may be reproduced, stored in a retrieval system, or transmitted in any form or by any means, electronic, mechanical, photocopying, recording or otherwise, without written permission from churchplantingdoctor.com
Any profits from the sale of this course will be used to promote theological education in the third world.
Scripture taken from the HOLY BIBLE, NEW INTERNATIONAL VERSION®.
Copyright © 1973, 1978, 1984, 2011 Biblica. Used by permission of Zondervan.

ISBN 978-1-7366426-8-9

Printed by ~~~~~~~~~~~~~~~

CONTENTS

INTRODUCTION TO CHURCH PLANTING

Jesus said to Peter in the Gospel of Matthew that He will build His Church, and that the Gates of Hell will not overcome it:

> *Matthew 16:18 (NIV)* "18 And I tell you that you are Peter, and on this Rock, **I will build my church, and the gates of Hades will not overcome it**. 19 I will give you the keys of the kingdom of heaven; whatever you bind on earth will be bound in heaven, and whatever you loose on earth will be loosed in heaven."

Our journey together will explore what we learned from the Word of God and through experience in Church Planting on 6 Continents and in over 75 nations. After training thousands of Church Leaders, over the past 35 years, I learnt that there are definite keys to successful Church Planting. Keys are principles, which, when applied, used and adhered to, should have a predetermined outcome. Godly Principles apply whether you believe them or don't. I trust that this book will be of assistance to you in understanding the way to a more successful and fruitful ministry in Church Planting. Church Planting is both exciting and challenging at the same time. It is an expression of one of the most biblical ways of evangelising and expanding the Kingdom of God.

May the Lord give us a spirit of understanding and knowledge as we take this journey. I will attempt developing an appreciation for the high call of God to ministry, understanding the power of prayer, the importance of developing leadership and attending to administrative systems.

May your heart be enlarged, and your vision expanded. My prayer is that you will be encouraged by the possibilities and that you will find yourself taking heart at the task before you.

In His Service and for His Glory!

Bishop Dr. Hendrik J. Vorster

1

THE CHALLENGE

Never in history has the task before us been so enormous and compelling! The immensity of the challenge, to preach and reach every tongue, tribe and nation with the Good News of Jesus Christ is increasing at disproportionate rates. If we consider the net world population growth, compared with the conversion rate within the Church, if we consider the moral depravity and falling away, if we consider the real financial economic position of nations, not to speak of the average person in the street, if we consider the health and welfare of people, if we consider the true educational level within the world compared to the tempo at which knowledge is increasing, we have to conclude that the task is huge!!

Never has the opportunity to make a tangible and sound difference been at such a premium as what it is now. We have an opportunity to make a difference, and I think it is time for those who can, who have, and are able, to dig down deep and go, or help those who can, to reach our generation with the Gospel of Jesus Christ.

The .... Challenge

Matthew 24:14 (KJV)"[14] And this gospel of the kingdom shall be preached in all the world for a witness unto all nations; and then shall the end come."

Revelation 5:8-10 (NIV) "[8] And when he had taken it, the four living creatures and the twenty-four elders fell down before the Lamb. Each one had a harp and they were holding golden bowls full of incense, which are the prayers of the saints [9] And they sang a new song: "You are worthy to take the scroll and to open its seals, because you were slain, and with your blood you purchased men for God from every tribe and language and people and nation.[10] You have made them to be a kingdom and priests to serve our God, and they will reign on the earth."

What is that commission to us as Believers?

Matthew 28:19-20 (KJV)"[19] Go ye therefore, and teach all nations, baptizing them in the name of the Father, and of the Son, and of the Holy Ghost: [20] Teaching them to observe all things whatsoever I have commanded you: and, lo, I am with you always, even unto the end of the world. Amen."

The Barna research group started a research project among professing Christians in 1993, which they published in December 2013, to determine the extent to which believers share their faith. Their research showed an alarming, and increasing, low level of participation of believers actually sharing their faith.

The challenge exists not only to spread the Word to the ends of the earth, but the researchers found, also to mobilise those within the Church to actually take up their responsibility and go and share. The challenge is therefore twofold, both in getting believers to share, as well as mobilising them to share.

John Daniel posted a research document in ChristianPost.com on July 12, 2013:

1. "..................................., of being ridiculed, disapproved and persecuted by the world, especially those who have authority over us parents, spouses and bosses,"

2. "Not feeling they are ...."

3. "Just wanting to keep their ...."

4. "Complacency, lack of ...., passion and laziness." 5. "Too many worry about being .... correct." 6. "Influenced by a .... culture."

7. "A lack of .... and don't know How to share."

8. "A feeling of not being .... Christians with .... faith."

9. "Few people .... what they said they believed in."

10. "They embrace .... beliefs."

11. "They don't know the .... clearly and rightly."

12. "They don't see the .... from Church leaders."

The .... Challenge

> Matthew 24:37-39 (NIV) "[37] As it was in the days of Noah, so it will be at the coming of the Son of Man. [38] For in the days before the flood, people were eating and drinking, marrying and giving in marriage, up to the day Noah entered the ark; [39] and they knew nothing about what would happen until the flood came and took them all away. That is how it will be at the coming of the Son of Man. "

To understand the context of Jesus' warning here in Matthew 24, we have to take a look back in Genesis when Noah was called upon to build an ark. He built an ark and he preached a message for people to make right with God.

> Genesis 6:5 (AMP) "[5] The Lord saw that the wickedness of man was great in the earth, and that every imagination and intention of all human thinking was only evil continually."

> Genesis 6:11-12 (AMP) "[11] The earth was depraved and putrid in God's sight, and the land was filled with violence (desecration, infringement, outrage, assault, and lust for power). [12] And God looked upon the world and saw how degenerate, debased, and vicious it was, for all humanity had corrupted their way upon the earth and lost their true direction."

These few verses give us a quick insight into what Jesus meant when He referred to the days of Noah. There existed an unhealthy environment of lust, greed, violence, desecration, viciousness, where every inclination and intention of all human thinking was only evil all the time.

> Genesis 6:8-9 (AMP)" [8] But Noah found grace (favor) in the eyes of the Lord. [9]This is the history of the generations of Noah. Noah was a just and righteous man, blameless in his [evil] generation; Noah walked [in habitual fellowship] with God."

The .... Challenge

Earlier in 2016, the global population topped to 7.4 Billion people. Net world population growth was around 78 million people in 2015.

If the average church size is .... people per congregation then we need more than a million new churches per year.

If the average Cell group or Home group is .... people, then we need just over 5,600,000 new Cell group leaders to accommodate and reach the annual net world population growth.

Matthew 9:37-38 [NIV] "The harvest is plentiful, but the workers are few! Ask the Lord of the Harvest, therefor, to send out workers into his harvest field."

The .... People Groups Challenge

A total of 6671 wholly Unreached People groups! We still have 3803 Partially Reached People groups. We still have 1106 Minimally Reached People groups, and 1679 formerly or falsely Reached people groups.

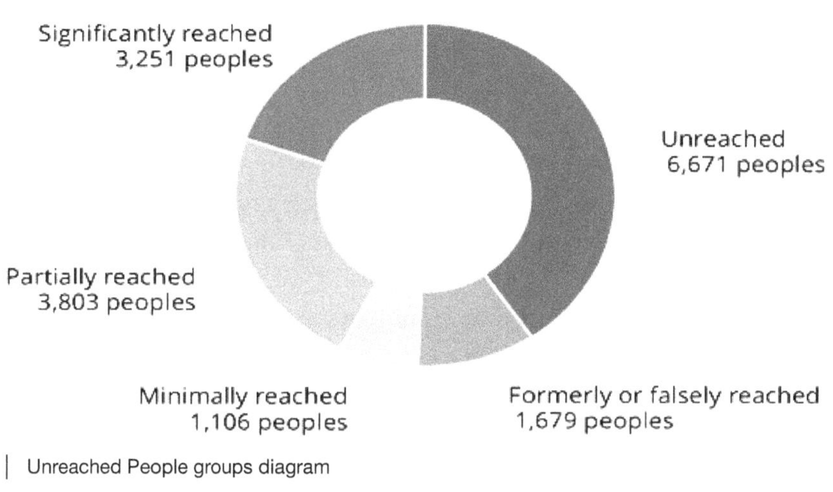

Unreached People groups diagram

The Urbanization ....

The ever-increasing amount of people flocking to urban areas calls for our urgent attention. We need a rethink on the way to reach urban people. The complexities around confined spaces, time restraints, work environments and cultures compete with our historical approaches of Church Planting. Learning from those who have been able to effectively reach their city dwellers should be at the forefront of our pursuits.

A report by the United Nations, Department of Economic and Social Affairs, Population Division (2014) reports as follows: - World Urbanisation Prospects: The 2014 Revision

- Globally, more people live in urban areas than in rural areas, with 54 per cent of the world's population residing in urban areas in 2014. In 1950, 30 per cent of the world's population was urban, and by 2050, 66 per cent of the world's population is projected to be urban.
- Just three countries—India, China and Nigeria— together are expected to account for 37 per cent of the projected growth of the world's urban population between 2014 and 2050. India is projected to add 404 million urban dwellers, China 292 million and Nigeria 212 million.
- Close to half of the world's urban dwellers reside in relatively small settlements of less than 500,000 inhabitants, while only around one in eight live in the 28 mega-cities with more than 10 million inhabitants.
- Tokyo is the world's largest city with an agglomeration of 38 million inhabitants, followed by Delhi with 25 million, Shanghai with 23 million, and Mexico City, Mumbai and São Paulo, each with around 21 million inhabitants. By 2030, the world is projected to have 41 mega-cities with more than 10 million inhabitants. Tokyo is projected to remain the world's largest city in 2030 with 37 million inhabitants, followed closely by Delhi where the population is projected to rise swiftly to 36 million. Several decades ago, most of the world's largest urban agglomerations were found in the more developed regions, but today's large cities are concentrated in the global South. The fastest- growing urban agglomerations are medium-sized cities and cities with less than 1 million inhabitants located in Asia and Africa.
- Some cities have experienced population decline in recent years. Most of these are located in the low- fertility countries

of Asia and Europe where the overall population is stagnant or declining. Economic contraction and natural disasters have contributed to population losses in some cities as well.

Jonah 4:11 (NIV) - [11] But Nineveh has more than a hundred and twenty thousand people who cannot tell their right hand from their left, and many cattle as well. Should I not be concerned about that great city?"

The .... demographical Challenge

It remains true that the most responsive people to receive Jesus as their Lord and Saviour come from the age group of under 15, and at present we have around 26% of young people in that age bracket.

The .... Challenge.

Sadly, not all migrations and people movements were the result of choice. Wars and political unrest, genocide, racial and religious wars caused many mass migrations throughout the ages. The result of these people displacements brought new opportunities and challenges. Many revivals came about as a result of these migrations.

The Book of Acts tells us that Jesus' original intention was that His disciples would be His witnesses both in Jerusalem, Judea, Samaria and the ends of the earth, however, we find them confined to Jerusalem until a persecution broke out, and as a result of this mass people migration or displacement, the gospel eventually spread, but this came by default and not by intention.

Acts 1:8 (NIV) - [8] But you will receive power when the Holy Spirit comes on you; and you will be my witnesses in Jerusalem, and in all Judea and Samaria, and to the ends of the earth."

Acts 8:1 (NIV) - The Church Persecuted and Scattered - [8:1] And Saul was there, giving approval to his death. On that day a great persecution broke out against the church at Jerusalem, and all except the apostles were scattered throughout Judea and Samaria.

Acts 8:4 (NIV) - Philip in Samaria - [4] Those who had been scattered preached the word wherever they went.

Acts 11:19-21 (NIV) -The Church in Antioch - [19] Now those who had been scattered by the persecution in connection with Stephen traveled as far as Phoenicia, Cyprus and Antioch, telling the message only to Jews. [20] Some of them, however, men from Cyprus and Cyrene, went to Antioch and began to speak to Greeks also, telling them the good news about the Lord Jesus. [21] The Lord's hand was with them, and a great number of people believed and turned to the Lord.

Today we have the Syrian migration. Millions have been displaced through war! We have the Ethiopian and Southern African migration resulting in major Xenophibian attacks whereby thousands of people are losing their lives. Just think of the hostilities between Muslim extremists and the Christians in Northern African countries like Nigeria. We have the Mexican migration into North America. Within Asia we have the constant migration of people attempting to flee their own to find a better life elsewhere.

Most effective form of evangelism

Dr. C. Peter Wagner, in his Book "Church Planting for a greater harvest" says: "the most effective methodology for evangelism is church planting." He goes on to say that his research shown that an average of 46 people come to the Lord through each and every new church that is planted. His research shows that the most effective methodology of evangelism is through Church Planting. May the Lord of the Harvest help us to work smarter and not just harder.

Conclusion

May we never cease to ask the Father for workers to bring in the harvest. The safest and most secure place to bring the harvest into is the local church. That local church might start as, or operate as a cell group, but that is where the harvest needs to be brought into. I believe God is calling more men and woman, to face the challenge for world evangelization, than what many seem to think. There might be people in your family, group, congregation, or even if you are a pastor reading this book, who actually sense the call of God on their lives. You might be the one whom God is challenging to take the challenge. Let's face the challenge before us and go and plant churches to reach our generation for Christ.

This brings us to the next Chapter on our Church Planting journey, responding and understanding the Call of God.

2

THE CALL TO CHURCH PLANTING

After years of research and study, I concluded, that the first, and most important step in the journey of planting a Church, is that you need to be called by God. The Bible is a compilation of men and woman who answered the call of God on their lives. All of them had to fulfil a Divine Purpose in the Salvatory Acts of God. He equipped each and every one of them with His Holy Spirit, who enabled them to carry out the calling with which He called them. Their obedience, submission and fulfillment of the Call are clearly applauded throughout Scripture. Each one's calling was different and unique, and even though there might be many similarities, or things that might, on the surface, seem to be common, their Calling and Purpose was uniquely different.

A wave of People responding to the Call of God

Over recent years I have noticed a new wave of men and woman responding to the Call of God. Of course, **in one sense, we are all called!** 1 Peter 2:10 tell us that **we have been called "out of darkness into the light."** Galatians 1:6 speak about being **called "into the grace of Jesus Christ"** which in essence means to be called unto salvation.

2 Thessalonians 2:13-14 (KJV)" [13] But we are bound to give thanks always to God for you, brethren beloved of the Lord, because God hath from the beginning chosen you to salvation through sanctification of the Spirit and belief of the truth: [14] Whereunto **he called you by our gospel**, to the obtaining of the glory of our Lord Jesus Christ."

Church Planting is quite a specified field. We will endeavour to explore the Calling of the person, the purpose for which God Calls, the Place to where He Calls, the Responsibilities of the Called, and the Enabling required for the Call to Church Planting.

The .... Calling of God

The writer to the Hebrews speaks of this High Calling in Hebrews 3:1-2 (NIV) and Hebrews 5:4-5.

Hebrews 3:1-2 (NIV.) "[1] Therefore, holy brothers and sisters, who share in **the heavenly calling**, fix your thoughts on Jesus, whom we acknowledge as **our apostle and high priest.** [2] **He was faithful to the one who appointed him**, just as Moses was faithful in all God's house."

Hebrews 5:4-5 (KJV) "[4] And no man taketh this honour unto himself, but **he that is called of God**, as was Aaron. [5] So also Christ glorified not himself to be made a high priest; but he that said unto him, Thou art my Son, today have I begotten thee."

A few things stand out for me in these two verses. In the first place, he speaks of a:

- (1) **"Heavenly calling."** This call seems to be a higher calling, yet he includes the brothers and sisters in his address, ***who share*** in the Heavenly Calling. The second thing that stands out for me is

- (2) **The Purpose** for which Jesus was called and appointed. We see that he was called to be "our Apostle and High Priest." In the third place, I see that
- (3) **God appointed Jesus** to that office or ministry, to which He was called. In the fourth place, I see that
- (4) **Jesus was faithful to the One who called and appointed Him**.

The message I take from this is that ***God Calls people, for a Specific Purpose, and upon answering the call, He appoints them in that ministry or office***. Those who are Called, have the responsibility to remain faithful to God who had given the Appointment to them!

The .... Call of God

It is absolutely essential that you affirm the Call of God upon your life. The Apostle Peter, in his second Epistle, exhorts us to affirm the Call of God, and I would say, the Purpose of God, in our lives.

> 2 Peter 1:10 (AMP) he says:"10 Because of this, brethren, be all the more solicitous and eager to **make sure (to ratify, to strengthen, to make steadfast) your calling and election**; for if you do this, you will never stumble or fall."

.. for the Call

The Apostle Paul gave this advice to the young disciple Timothy that he should study to show himself approved by God. Preparing ourselves for the task before us is an essential part of being greatly used by the Lord.

> 2 Timothy 2:15 (KJV)" [15] Study to show thyself

approved unto God, a workman that needeth not to be ashamed, rightly dividing the word of truth."

2 Timothy 2:15 (AMP)" [15] Study and be eager and do your utmost to present yourself to God approved (tested by trial), a workman who has no cause to be ashamed, correctly analyzing and accurately dividing [rightly handling and skillfully teaching] the Word of Truth."

2 Timothy 1:5 (NIV)" [5] I have been reminded of your sincere faith, which first lived in your grandmother Lois and in your mother Eunice and, I am persuaded, now lives in you also."

Called for a ....

We learn from Romans 8:28 and Ephesians 1:11 that God calls for a purpose. There is always purpose in God's call upon our lives!

Romans 8:28 (KJV)" [28] And we know that all things work together for good to them that love God, to them who are the called according to his purpose."

Ephesians 1:11 (KJV)" [11] In whom also we have obtained an inheritance, being predestinated according to the purpose of him who worketh all things after the counsel of his own will:"

You might recall that when God called Jeremiah, He told Him that He placed this Call, to be a Prophet, upon his life before he was born. For Church Planters, God's calling of men and woman, is to serve primarily in **the Apostolic or Evangelistic Office**, or as the Message Bible says: "as **missionaries**."

> Jeremiah 1:5 (NIV)" [5] "Before I formed you in the womb, I knew you, before you were born, I set you apart, **I appointed you as a prophet to the nations**."

.... for the Call

Those whom God calls, He also **anoints with special gifts** to enable them to be determined blessings to the Church, but also, to endure the hardship and persecutions that accompany this ministry. At the beginning of Jesus' earthly ministry, He received the empowerment of the Holy Spirit.

> Matthew 3:16 (NIV) "[16] As soon as Jesus was baptized, he went up out of the water. At that moment heaven was opened, and he saw the Spirit of God descending like a dove and lighting on him."

The Gospel of Luke goes on to say that Jesus was full of the spirit when He was led into the wilderness to be tempted by the devil.

> Luke 4:1 (NIV)" [4:1] Jesus, full of the Holy Spirit, returned from the Jordan and was led by the Spirit in the desert,"

Jesus affirmed this Anointing from on High when He went into the Synagogue on the Sabbath day.

> Luke 4:18 (NIV)" [18] "**The Spirit of the Lord is on me, because** he has anointed **me to preach good news to the poor.** He has sent me to proclaim freedom for the prisoners and recovery of sight for the blind, to release the oppressed,"

> Acts 10:38 (NIV) "[38] how **God anointed Jesus of Nazareth with the Holy Spirit and power**, and how he went around doing good and healing all who were

under the power of the devil, because God was with him."

Acts 1:4-5 (NIV)" [4] On one occasion, while he was eating with them, he gave them this command: "Do not leave Jerusalem, but wait for the gift my Father promised, which you have heard me speak about. [5] For John baptized with water, but in a few days, you will be baptized with the Holy Spirit."

Acts 1:8 (NIV)" [8] But you will receive power when the Holy Spirit comes on you; and you will be my witnesses in Jerusalem, and in all Judea and Samaria, and to the ends of the earth."

The .... Calling

I see that Jesus first called a number of people to be His followers, and then subsequent to their faithful following, He appointed some as Apostles. I see an order in which the Heavenly Call of God works. ***First,*** He calls people, and ***then*** upon their yielding, obedience and faithfulness, he appoints them to one of the Offices, such as those named in Ephesians 4:11.

Ephesians 4:11 (NIV) "So Christ himself gave some to be apostles, some to be prophets, some to be evangelists, and some to be pastors and teachers,"

Jesus first called into Himself Disciples to follow Him in Matthew 4 verses 19-22:

Matthew 4:19-22 (NIV) "Come, follow me," Jesus said, "and I will send you out to fish for people." **At once they left their nets and followed him**. Going on from there, he saw two other brothers, James, son of Zebedee and his brother John. They were in a boat with their father Zebedee, preparing their nets. Jesus called them, and immediately they left the boat and their **father and followed him.**"

Mark 3:13-18 (NIV) "[13] Jesus went up on a mountainside and called to him those he wanted, and they came to him. [14] He appointed twelve — designating them apostles — that they might be with him and that he might send them out to preach [15] and to have authority to drive out demons. [16] These are the twelve he appointed: Simon (to whom he gave the name Peter); [17] James son of Zebedee and his brother John (to them he gave the name Boanerges, which means Sons of Thunder); [18] Andrew, Philip, Bartholomew, Matthew, Thomas, James son of Alphaeus, Thaddaeus, Simon the Zealot."

Luke 6:12-13 (KJV)" [12] And it came to pass in those days, that he went out into a mountain to pray, and continued all night in prayer to God. [13] And when it was day, **he called unto him his disciples: and of them he chose twelve, whom also he named apostles**;"

Luke 6:17 (KJV)" [17] And he came down with them, and stood in the plain, and **the company of his disciples,** and a great multitude of people out of all Judaea and Jerusalem, and from the sea coast of Tyre and Sidon, which came to hear him, and to be healed of their diseases;"

Ephesians 4:8 says: "8 this is why it says: "*When He ascended on high, He took many captives and gave gifts to his people*." The Greek word used for "gifts" is the word "χαϱιτοω" - "charitoo;" from the root word "charis"; to grace, or to indue with special honor: — to be highly favoured." These, highly favoured people, have been given as gifts to the Body of Christ, to equip them. Ephesians 4:11-13 concludes the statement in verse 8, and says:

> Ephesians 4:11-13 (NIV) "11 So Christ himself gave the apostles, the prophets, the evangelists, the pastors and teachers, 12 to equip his people for works of service, so that the body of Christ may be built up, 13 until we all reach unity in the faith and in the knowledge of the Son of God and become mature, attaining to the whole measure of the fullness of Christ."

.. Call

> Acts 16:6-10 (NIV)" [6] Paul and his companions traveled throughout the region of Phrygia and Galatia, having been **kept by the Holy Spirit from preaching** the word in the province of Asia. [7] When they came to the border of Mysia, they tried to enter Bithynia, but the Spirit **of Jesus would not allow them to.** [8] So they passed by Mysia and went down to Troas. [9] During the night Paul had a vision of a man of Macedonia standing and begging him, "Come over to Macedonia and help us." [10] After Paul had seen the vision, we got ready at once to leave for Macedonia, concluding that God had called us to preach the gospel to them."

> John 4:34 (NIV) "[34] "My food," said Jesus, "is to do the will of him who sent me and to finish his work.

> John 6:38 (NIV) "[38] For I have come down from heaven not to do my will but to do the will of him who sent me.

John 5:19 (NIV) "[19] Jesus gave them this answer: "I tell you the truth, the Son can do nothing by himself; he can do only what he sees his Father doing, because whatever the Father does the Son also does.

John 5:30 (NIV) "[30] By myself I can do nothing; I judge only as I hear, and my judgment is just, for I seek not to please myself but him who sent me.

Romans 8:14 (KJV) "[14] For as many as are led by the Spirit of God, they are the sons of God.

The .... and .... Call

Jesus came and declared His assigned people group. On one occasion, as we read in Matthew 15:24, a Canaanite woman begged Him to heal and restore her daughter, He declared that He was "**only sent to the Lost sheep of Israel**."

Matthew 15:24 (NIV)" [24] He answered, "I was sent only to the lost sheep of Israel."

Matthew 10:5-6 (NIV)" [5] These twelve Jesus sent out with the following instructions: "**Do not go** among the Gentiles or enter any town of the Samaritans. [6] **Go rather to the lost sheep of Israel**."

The Apostles Peter and Paul carried upon their lives different purposes. Galatians highlight for us the specific purpose of this heavenly Call of God upon their lives.

Galatians 2:7-9 (NIV)" [7] On the contrary, they saw that I had been entrusted with the task of preaching the gospel to the Gentiles, just as Peter had been to the Jews. [8] For God, who was at work in the ministry of Peter as an apostle to the Jews, was also at work in

> my ministry as an apostle to the Gentiles. [9] James, Peter and John, those reputed to be pillars, gave me and Barnabas the right hand of fellowship when they recognized the grace given to me. They agreed that we should go to the Gentiles, and they to the Jews."

Both concluded, as their ministry profile developed, that God assigned and called them specifically to preach the Gospel to an assigned group of people. So, even though the instruction is to '**go into all the world and preach the Gospel to all nations,**' we can and should only go where He leads, for that is where you will experience the grace to succeed.

Conclusion

I pray you too will be one of this new generation of Church Planters who will courageously follow the call of the Lord to wherever He might lead you, to do whatever He desires you to do, to the people group or nations to whom He calls you to, to fulfil His Call.

We are so privileged to be called and to participate in this High Calling of God. Make every day count.

Use every opportunity to learn, experiment and to obediently follow the voice of the Holy Spirit.

3

PHASES OF CHURCH PLANTING

There are basically five phases to planting a dynamic Church, three of which happens prior to the Church being constituted, and one after her going public.

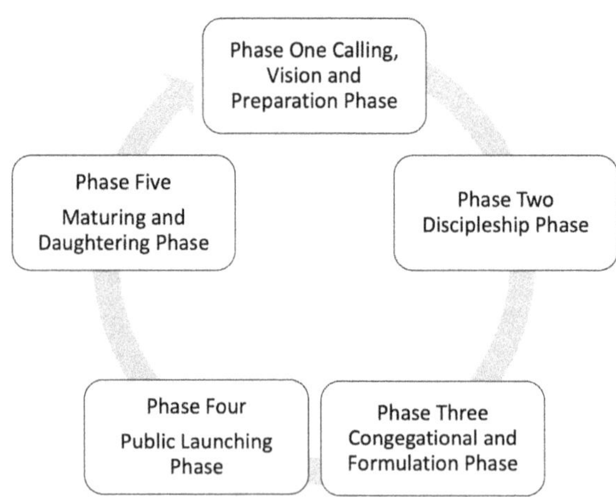

Phases of Church Planting Diagram

1). Calling, Vision and Preparation Phase

Phase One describes the **Calling, Vision and Preparation** Phase, where we ensure that we depart on this exciting journey with a clear Call of God upon our lives, a Holy Spirit Inspired Vision, the Empowerment of the Holy Spirit, well established Spiritual Disciplines, and under the Discipleship of a Godly Discipler.

2). The Discipleship Phase

Phase Two describes the **Discipleship** Phase. The Discipleship Phase marks the first steps in planting a Fruit-producing, multipliable Church by finding our Disciples, our worthy men and woman, and this is a key landmark during this phase. The Discipleship Phase is also the phase where we develop and establish our God-ordained DNA through the process of discipleship. If you do this right, it most certainly guarantees success.

During this phase we also mobilize our disciples from learners to practitioners. Another landmark during this phase is that we put things we've learnt into practice, and one of the key steps towards a '***fruit- producing***' life is leading someone to the Lord, baptizing them, as well as having a consistent, life ***share-able*** relationship in Christ. This phase is also landmarked by our disciples gathering their disciples into groups for effective ministry, teaching and discipleship them.

3). The Congregating, and the Formulizing of the Discipleship groups, Phase

Phase Three describes the **congregating, and the formulizing of the Discipleship groups**.

Some of the key landmarks during this phase are the formulation of the Church constitution, refining the Church structure, and appointing office bearers. During this phase we organize the Discipleship Group Leaders, by appointing some Elders, some as Deacons, and some into key administrative and organizational roles. Establishing a sound Administrative system and appointing Key staff is essential during this phase.

Attention is given to formulizing the liturgy for the congregational services. Until this point most, if not all, of the growth came through personal evangelism, however, during this phase corporate harvesting events are planned and developed to not just reach our Jerusalem, but also our Judea, Samaria and the ends of the earth. We organize our disciples into body ministry areas. During this phase look for the right place to bring everyone together. It is essential to effective Church Planting that we have each of these in place to truly have a New Testament Church foundation to build upon. This phase is also defined by the development and implementation of systems to maintain the health and welfare, and continued growth of the Church. (Systems are defined in the Chapter on systems.)

4). Church' public launching Phase

Phase Four describes th**e Church' public launching** Phase. This phase is landmarked by the Discipleship Groups congregating for Weekly Worship, observing the Sacraments and Celebration. During this phase we start seeing this body of Believers going public as a unified Body where each one does its part to build the Church up. During this phase the Church mobilizes herself into a corporate harvesting machine. By maintaining the DNA of Discipleship and keeping its focus on seeking and saving the lost, the church will traject herself on a pathway of continued growth. You will find Timothy's raised, Paul's released, and the Kingdom of God expanding in various and wonderful ways.

5). Maturing and Daughtering Phase

Phase Five describes the **Maturing and Daughtering** Phase. Healthy churches reproduce, and this is mostly observed by their ability to continue to plant new churches. Instead of being alarmed by some seemingly wanting to break away to start their own ministries, rather embrace the cycle of seeing our spiritual sons and daughters mature and coming ministers and leaders in their own right. Some will stay with you and some will want to go. If you observe their destiny before they do, you could actually make the whole process of multiplication a pleasant one and release them in a God-honouring way! Churches need to multiply to continue to grow.

4

TWELVE CHARACTERISTICS DEFINING DYNAMIC CHURCH PLANTING LEADERS

Here is a few characteristics, shared by dynamic Church Planting Leaders. These are not conclusive, however for the purpose of our study they will be very helpful in affirming how God has prepared you to be a next generational Church Planting Leader. Also, these are not in any specific order, but definitely all common among the greatest leaders, both in New Testament days as well as in our day.

1. ....

The primary attitude for every dynamic Church planter is that of obedience. The same heart attitude that allowed Joshua and Caleb to enter into the Promised Land is also the same heart attitude that allowed New Testament Believers to possess their Promised Lands. The Believers had the same Faith to obey God's Call.

Jesus taught His Disciples both the importance of hearing God's Word and obedience to do it.

> Luke 11:28 (NIV) "28 He replied, "Blessed rather are those who hear the word of God and obey it."

The Apostles walked in this same obedience to the Word of the Lord to them.

> Acts 5:29 (NIV) "29 Peter and the other apostles replied: "We must obey God rather than human beings!"

2. Prayer and ....

Spiritual disciplines greatly advance our Church Planting efforts. Jesus started His ministry after a period of Fasting and Prayer. We see that He prayed often and at times even spent whole nights in prayer.

The Disciples were men of prayer. One of the hallmarks of the New Testament Believers was that of meeting regularly for prayer.

> Acts 1:14 (NIV) "14 They all joined together constantly in prayer, along with the women and Mary the mother of Jesus, and with his brothers."

> Acts 2:42 (NIV) "42 They devoted themselves to the apostles' teaching and to fellowship, to the breaking of bread and to prayer."

Every decision was bathed in prayer prior to them pursuing any thing. It was after a night of prayer that Jesus chose His Disciples. It was during a time of Fasting and Prayer in the Church in Antioch that the Holy Spirit spoke and gave Barnabas and Saul their "Great Commission."

> Acts 13:2-3 (NIV) 2 While they were worshiping the Lord and fasting, the Holy Spirit said, "Set apart for me Barnabas and Saul for the work to which I have called them." 3 So after they had fasted and prayed, they placed their hands on them and sent them off.

One of the hallmarks of most, if not all, dynamic Church Planting Leaders is their practice of Fasting and Disciplined Prayer lives.

3. .... Preaching and the Teaching of the Apostles

The Apostles made a deep commitment to preach and teach sound biblical doctrine, as inspired by the Holy Spirit.

> Acts 2:42 (NIV) "42 They devoted themselves to the apostles' teaching and to fellowship, to the breaking of bread and to prayer."

The Apostles impressed their disciples to preach sound doctrine.

> Titus 2:1 (NIV) "1 You, however, must teach what is appropriate to sound doctrine."

> 2 Timothy 4:2 (NIV) "2 Preach the word; be prepared in season and out of season; correct, rebuke and encourage—with great patience and careful instruction."

One of the stark differences I've seen between many popular preachers and those who really impact and advance the Kingdom of God, is their ability to preach a sound Gospel message based on the Word and from the Word. Those who truly advance the Kingdom of God are those who preach the Word of God.

4. Holy ....: The primary person and partner for successful Church Planting is the Holy Spirit. No journey in Church Planting is possible without the powerful work and ministration of the Holy Spirit.

> Luke 4:18-19 (NIV) 18 "The Spirit of the Lord is on me, because he has anointed me to proclaim good news to the poor. He has sent me to proclaim freedom for the prisoners and recovery of sight for the blind, to set the

oppressed free, 19 to proclaim the year of the Lord's favor."

Acts 10:38 (NIV) "38 how God anointed Jesus of Nazareth with the Holy Spirit and power, and how he went around doing good and healing all who were under the power of the devil, because God was with him."

The Gospel of John ascribe many and great things to the Holy Spirit. Jesus promised that the Father would send the Holy Spirit to those obey Him and keep His commandments.

John 14:26 (NIV) "26 But the Advocate, the Holy Spirit, whom the Father will send in my name, will teach you all things and will remind you of everything I have said to you."

Acts 8:29 (NIV) "29 The Spirit told Philip, "Go to that chariot and stay near it."

The result of this one act of obedience of Philip was that an Ethiopian Eunuch was saved, baptised and he saw Philip translated.

Whilst the Church in Antioch was fasting and praying the Holy Spirit spoke and gave Barnabas and Saul their "Great Commission" which ultimately resulted in many churches being planted in Asia through the lives of these obedient Apostles.

Acts 13:2, 4. (NIV) "2 While they were worshiping the Lord and fasting, the Holy Spirit said, "Set apart for me Barnabas and Saul for the work to which I have called them." 4 The two of them, sent on their way by the Holy Spirit, went down to Seleucia and sailed from there to Cyprus."

5. .... and Wonders.

The early church grew as they witnessed the powerful working of the Holy Spirit in the lives of the Apostles and Believers. Jesus promised, "These signs shall follow those who believe." As Believers discover and avail themselves to the Holy Spirit Gifts inside of them, they become witnesses of this Mighty Working Power of God.

Acts 2:43 (NIV) "43 Everyone was filled with awe at the many wonders and signs performed by the apostles."

6. Apostolic ....: The early Church embraced the apostolic and being an apostolic people. Jesus first introduced the idea of the Apostolic when He chose, from among His Disciples, twelve Apostles.

> Luke 6:13 (NIV) "13 When morning came, he called his disciples to him and chose twelve of them, whom he also designated apostles:"

These Apostles held their designation with pride and ultimately took the Message of Christ to the ends of the earth.

The Apostolic ministry continued throughout the New Testament Church era. We see that Paul enforces the notion in his letters to the Romans, Ephesians and Corinthians. He refers to himself and Timothy as Apostles.

> Ephesians 4:11 (NIV) "11 So Christ himself gave the apostles, the prophets, the evangelists, the pastors and teachers,"

> 1 Thessalonians 1:1 (NIV) "1 Paul, Silas and Timothy, To the church of the Thessalonians in God the Father and the Lord Jesus Christ: Grace and peace to you."

7. Prophetic: The Prophetic Word is present in every successful Church plant.

> Ephesians 4:11 NIV "11 So Christ himself gave the apostles, the prophets, the evangelists, the pastors and teachers,"

> Ephesians 2:20 NIV "20 built on the foundation of the apostles and prophets, with Christ Jesus himself as the chief cornerstone."

8. Pastoral: Caring for the harvest is as important as reaching them.

> Ephesians 4:11 NIV "11 So Christ himself gave the apostles, the prophets, the evangelists, the pastors and teachers,"

9. Evangelistic: The lifeblood of every work is her successful reaching and assimilating lost people.

> Ephesians 4:11 NIV "11 So Christ himself gave the apostles, the prophets, the evangelists, the pastors and teachers,"

10. Discipleship: Discipleship stands central to bringing people to maturity and fruitfulness.

11. Servanthood: Serving the poor, orphans, elderly and widows will validate our faith.

12. Biblical structures: Organizational structures provide stability to growing church movements, not for lording it over but for smooth fulfillment of the purpose of God.

5

PHASE ONE – ...., VISION AND PREPARATION PHASE

In Church Planting it is true that a Called Servant of God, combined with a Holy Spirit inspired Vision, empowered by the Holy Spirit, living a Spiritually Disciplined, relational life in Christ, under the Discipleship of a Mature Follower of Jesus Christ, will most certainly advance the prospects for successful and efficient Discipleship and ultimately dynamic Church Planting. Having the right man in the right location, at the right time, will most certainly provide for Kingdom advancing successes.

During this initial phase of Church Planting, we lay a deep and solid foundation upon which we could truly build a ministry that will greatly advance the Kingdom of God, as well as endure the test of time. The diligence we apply in making thorough preparations will ensure that the Vision God gave us will be accomplished.

a. ....

Step One is to make your Calling sure and Fast. We need to make sure that we are called to lead the planting of a Church. Everyone is called to be part of Church Planting, but not all carry that anointing to lead the planting of a new church. The Apostle Peter said in his second Epistle that the brothers should "make their calling and election sure."

> 2 Peter 1:10 KJV "10 Wherefore the rather, brethren, give diligence to make your calling and election sure: for if ye do these things, ye shall never fall."

> 2 Timothy 1:9 KJV "9 Who hath saved us, and called us with an holy calling, not according to our works, but according to his own purpose and grace, which was given us in Christ Jesus before the world began,"

The writer to the Hebrews speaks of this "High Calling" in Hebrews 3 verses 1-2 (NIV) and Hebrews 5 verses 4-5:

> Hebrews 3:1-2 (NIV.) "[1] Therefore, holy brothers and sisters, who share in the heavenly calling, fix your thoughts on Jesus, whom we acknowledge as our apostle and high priest. [2] He was faithful to the one who appointed him, just as Moses was faithful in all God's house."

> Hebrews 5:4-5 (KJV) [4] And no man take this honour unto himself, but he that is called of God, as was Aaron. [5] So also Christ glorified not himself to be made an high priest; but he that said unto him, Thou art my Son, to day have I begotten thee.

The Apostle Paul, in his letter to the Romans, says that we are "Called for a purpose." Things work out for those who live according to the Call and Purpose of God on their lives.

> Romans 8:28 KJV "28 And we know that all things work together for good to them that love God, to them who are the called according to his purpose."

Although this Scripture is a Word of encouragement to every Believer, it does emphasise that there is a Divinely Inspired Purpose for the Call of God upon our lives.

To prepare oneself for a lifetime of ministry, one has to affirm that you are Called of God to pioneer a New Church.

b...

Step two is making sure that you pursue God's Vision and not your own. The Power of Vision and having a Vision from God is incredibly important for successful Church Planting.

Every new season starts with a vision. The word of God teaches us that: "Without a Vision people perish" It is important that we keep the example and teaching of our Lord Jesus in the forefront of our hearts and minds when He repeatedly emphasized the fact that He was only doing what His Father commissioned and assigned for Him to do. We should take earnest heed to this advice and example if we want to see dynamic Churches planted and multiplied through our lives and ministries.

> John 5:30 KJV "30 I can of mine own self do nothing: as I hear, I judge: and my judgment is just; because I seek not mine own will, but the will of the Father which hath sent me."

> John 5:19-20 AMP "19 So Jesus answered them by saying, I assure you, most solemnly I tell you, the Son is able to do nothing of Himself (of His own accord); but He is able to do only what He sees the Father doing, for whatever the Father does is what the Son does in the same way [in His turn]. 20 The Father dearly loves the Son and discloses to (shows) Him everything that He Himself does. And He will disclose to Him (let Him see) greater things yet than these, so that you may marvel and be full of wonder and astonishment."

Having a Vision from God, and constantly doing what the Lord shows you to do will ensure a lifetime of fulfilled ministry. The Apostle Paul found the truth of this in his ministry when he made many attempts to preach the Word of God in regions outside of the specific assignment and instruction of God.

> Acts 16:6-10 AMP "6 And Paul and Silas passed through the territory of Phrygia and Galatia, having been forbidden by the Holy Spirit to proclaim the Word in [the province of] Asia.7 And when they had come opposite Mysia, they tried to go into Bithynia, but the Spirit of Jesus did not permit them. 8 So passing by Mysia, they went down to Troas. 9 [There] a vision appeared to Paul in the night: a man from Macedonia stood pleading with him and saying, Come over to Macedonia and help us! 10 And when he had seen the vision, we [including Luke] at once endeavoured to go on into Macedonia, confidently inferring that God had called us to proclaim the glad tidings (Gospel) to them."

This portion clearly outlines to us the paramount importance of pursuing God's Vision for dynamic Church Planting. It was there, in one of the towns of Macedonia, in Philippi, where he straight away met Lydia, the dealer in purple dyed clothing, stayed in her house, and from there the Gospel spread throughout the entire region.

Having a clear vision from God before you venture into planting a new church is essential. The Church is His and He has a plan of how He desires to reach every man and woman on this planet. He reveals this plan to us through visions and dreams.

c. Wait for ....

Step Three is waiting to be endued with Power from on High before you start. Jesus, after His Baptism in water and the Baptism with the Holy Spirit, went into the desert for a 40 day Fasting and

Prayer time. This period was by all measures an empowering time for Him since we see that from that combined period of Fasting and Prayer, and receiving the empowerment of the Holy Spirit, He came forth with Power, and Signs and Wonders followed Him.

> Mark 1:13-28 KJV "13 And he was there in the wilderness
> forty days, tempted of Satan; and was with the wild
> beasts; and the angels ministered unto him. 14 Now
> after that John was put in prison, Jesus came into
> Galilee, preaching the gospel of the kingdom of God,
> 15 And saying, The time is fulfilled, and the kingdom
> of God is at hand: repent ye, and believe the gospel.

One of the remarkable things we see, when Jesus started His earthly ministry, was the miracles that followed His preaching. He healed many and delivered them from evil spirits because God was with Him.

> Mark 1: 21-23 KJV "27 And they were all amazed, in so
> much that they questioned among themselves, saying,
> What thing is this? What new doctrine is this? For
> with authority commanded he even the unclean
> spirits, and they do obey him. 28 And immediately
> his fame spread abroad throughout all the region
> round about Galilee."

Jesus demonstrated and gave us an example to follow. First, be equipped, and empowered by the Holy Spirit, before you start your ministry. This is the same message that He not only modelled, but also commanded His Disciples to follow. He clearly instructed them not to leave Jerusalem until they received the empowerment from on High.

> Acts 1:4-5 KJV "4 And, being assembled together with
> them, commanded them that they should not depart
> from Jerusalem, but wait for the promise of the
> Father, which, saith he, ye have heard of me. 5 For

> John truly baptized with water; but ye shall be baptized with the Holy Ghost not many days hence."

The Apostolic Church Leaders modelled this kind of waiting before they went out. In the Church in Antioch, even after the Holy Spirit spoke and commissioned Barnabas and Saul, they first fasted and prayed, and only afterwards they laid their hands on them and sent them out.

> Acts 13:2-4 AMP "2 While they were worshiping the Lord and fasting, the Holy Spirit said, Separate now for Me Barnabas and Saul for the work to which I have called them. 3 Then after fasting and praying, they put their hands on them and sent them away. 4 So then, being sent out by the Holy Spirit, they went down to Seleucia, and from [that port] they sailed away to Cyprus."

Dynamic Church Planting takes place when we do things God's way and when we patiently wait for His empowerment before we go. The very thing that defines us as men and woman of God is the Anointing we carry upon our lives. Be sure to not go until you've received that empowerment.

d. Spiritual ....

Step Four is to ensure that you have well-developed Spiritual Disciplines. Spiritual Disciplines are both important and necessary for our spiritual growth as well as keeping us empowered for a lifetime of ministry.

There are a number of Spiritual Disciplines. All of these Spiritual Disciplines will be discussed in my book "The Values and Disciplines of the Kingdom of God," but suffice to mention in this Chapter that the disciplines of Fasting and Prayer, Reading and meditating upon the Word of God, Worship, Witnessing, Contentment, Simplicity, Submission and Obedience, are some of the most important disciplines to develop.

If some, or all, of these mentioned disciplines are not already well established in your life, may I recommend that you start today, to put into place a priority and schedule of 1-2 hours per day, every day of the week, where you intentionally encounter with the Father, His Son and the Holy Spirit. My recommendation, if you are new to this, is that you start reading at least 5 Psalms, 1 Chapter in Proverbs, and 1 Book in the New Testament. Church Planters are predominantly early adopters, and therefor need to be at the forefront of High-Capacity Learning and adoption.

You will never be able to reproduce what you don't already have well established in your own life first. These, among many, form the solid spiritual foundation to ensure that you maintain the anointing of God upon your life as well as keep you in step and in touch with what God is saying and wanting to do, in and through you. It is by building these Spiritual disciplines into your life that you will keep yourself in and out of season bearing good and lasting fruit.

Step 5 is to ask God for a Discipler, unless you've already been approached to be Discipled. The fifth most important step to take in preparing to plant dynamic Churches is having a Discipler who will help and guide you to accomplish the vision God has given you.

> ***"A Discipler is someone who has been where you want to go, has the qualities, and character, you desire to have established in your life, and is willing to help you to reach your full potential, and fulfil your God-given goal."***

Biblically, I see that, in most cases, if not all, it is the Discipler who approaches the Disciple and then the Disciple has an option whether to follow or not. Elijah approached Elisha. Jesus called His Disciples to disciple them. The Apostle Paul was such a Discipler to many and he serves as a great example of one who was found, discipled, and then went on to fulfill His God-given purpose and did the same with many other disciples.

> 1 Kings 19:19-20 NIV "19 So Elijah went from there and found Elisha son of Shaphat. He was plowing with twelve yoke of oxen, and he himself was driving the twelfth pair. Elijah went up to him and threw his cloak around him. 20 Elisha then left his oxen and ran after Elijah."

Another example come from the Lord Jesus Himself when He called His Disciples to follow Him.

> Matthew 4:18-20 NIV "18 As Jesus was walking beside the Sea of Galilee, he saw two brothers, Simon called Peter and his brother Andrew. They were casting a net into the lake, for they were fishermen. 19 "Come, follow me," Jesus said, "and I will send you out to fish for people." 20 At once they left their nets and followed him."

Barnabas went to Tarsus where he called Saul (Paul) to follow him.

> Acts 11:25-26 NIV "25 Then Barnabas went to Tarsus to look for Saul, 26 and when he found him, he brought him to Antioch. So for a whole year Barnabas and Saul met with the church and taught great numbers of people. The disciples were called Christians first at Antioch."

When the Apostle Paul went on his way he went to Lystra and called Timothy to be his disciple.

Timothy followed Paul and we see that the Word of God spread throughout the whole region.

> Acts 16:1-5 NIV "1 Paul came to Derbe and then to Lystra, where a disciple named Timothy lived, whose mother was Jewish and a believer but whose father was a Greek. 2 The believers at Lystra and Iconium spoke well of him. 3 Paul wanted to take him along on the journey, so he circumcised him because of the Jews who lived in that area, for they all knew that his father was a Greek. 4 As they travelled from town to town, they delivered the decisions reached by the apostles and elders in Jerusalem for the people to obey. 5 So the churches were strengthened in the faith and grew daily in numbers."

Jesus called us to "***Go***" and to make "***Disciples***" of all nations. We see this pattern modelled throughout the Pastoral Epistles with frequent phrases like "***follow me as I follow Christ***" or "***follow my example***" or "you became models to the church." Every single Pastoral Epistles is built on the model Christ set before them.

They obeyed God's Call to make Disciples and so, through their example, led and discipled many. It was this foundational pattern that allowed the New Testament Church to grow and in relatively a short space of time they won their entire world for Christ, and even infiltrated and reached the entire Roman Empire.

This all came as a result of disciples being discipled well. We will never be able to develop the DNA of Discipleship in our churches unless and until we ourselves submit ourselves to be developed and discipled by a Godly Discipler.

In this regard, I learned a wonderful lesson from the Word when I was still a young man, in Matthew 20 verses 26-28:

> Matthew 20:26-28 (NIV) "26 Not so with you. Instead, whoever wants to become great among you must be your servant, 27 and whoever wants to be first must be your slave— 28 just as the Son of Man did not come to be served, but to serve, and to give his life as a ransom for many."

This Scripture taught me to "Serve my way up." I sought opportunities to serve great men and woman of God, and whilst sitting at their feet to learn from them and follow in their footsteps, God grew and developed me into what I am today. By being a servant to men and woman of God it brought me close enough that I could learn and observe the values of the Kingdom of God in operation. This step will put you ahead of any peer. Submission to a Godly Discipler will bring you to a place of making authentic disciples yourself.

6

PHASE TWO - DISCIPLESHIP

Let us take a moment and briefly look at the steps we need to take in Phase Two to establish a fruit- producing, disciple-making multiplying movement. I say briefly since this represents only a synoptic overview at this point.

For the purpose of this book, and this discussion on phases, it is important that we pursue the most expedient way of planting dynamic churches.

John Maxwell says:

"Everything rises and falls on Leadership."

In regards to planting dynamic churches, I say:

"Church planting rises and falls on Discipleship."

There are basically ***four steps*** in this ***Discipleship Phase***.

Step One - Evangelise and Preach

Step Two - Finding "Worthy Men."

Step Three - Disciple "Worthy Men."

Step Four - Gather the "Worthy Men" in Groups.

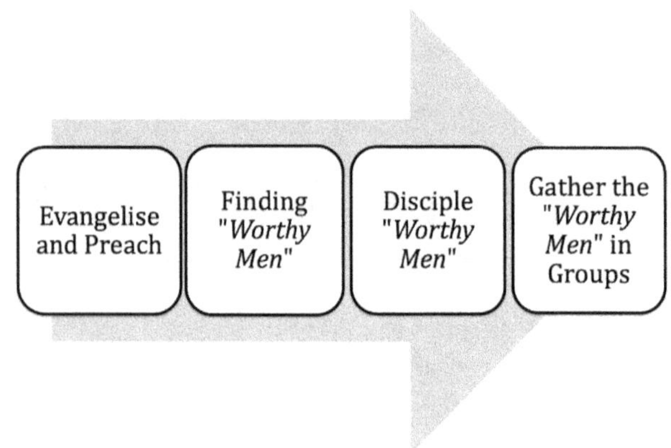

| Phase Two of Church Planting Diagram

Step One - Evangelising and preaching the Word of God.

Step 1 is to start evangelising and preaching the Word of God where God called you to go and plant a church. When both John and Jesus started their ministries, they both started by preaching the Message of Repentance.

> Luke 3:2-3 (NIV) "2 …the word of God came to John ... 3 He went into all the country around the Jordan, preaching a baptism of repentance for the forgiveness of sins."

> Matthew 4:17 (NIV) 17 From that time on Jesus began to preach, "Repent, for the kingdom of heaven has come near."

Phase Two of planting Dynamic churches start when we evangelise and preach the message God gave us, in the place where He assigned to us to go.

Where do we evangelise and preach?

Example in Jesus' ministry.

Jesus started His ministry by preaching everywhere and in the Synagogues. Everywhere meant in the markets, in the countryside, next to the sea of Galilee, and in the homes of many. When you go with the specific purpose of evangelising and preaching, you will find yourself at the right place at the right time most of the time.

This is what the Apostle Paul did after receiving his "***Macedonian Call***." He went and looked for a place to pray, and that is where he started sharing the Word. This also the place where He found a "Worthy" woman in whose house they lodged for a while whilst preaching the Word in her house.

> Acts 16:13-15 (NIV) 13 On the Sabbath we went outside the city gate to the river, where we expected to find a place of prayer. We sat down and began to speak to the women who had gathered there. 14 One of those listening was a woman from the city of Thyatira named Lydia, a dealer in purple cloth. She was a worshiper of God. The Lord opened her heart to respond to Paul's message. 15 When she and the members of her household were baptized, she invited us to her home. "If you consider me a believer in the Lord," she said, "come and stay at my house." And she persuaded us.

This is one of many beautiful examples of dynamic church planting. A Called man of God, sent out by the Will of God from a local Church, by the Holy Spirit, and Full of the Holy Spirit, with a Heavenly Assignment, and the result is a new church is planted.

Wherever God called you to go, go with the message that God

placed in your heart, seek a place where you can sit down and share that message. If it is a Message from God, and you are where He sent you, then you will find open hearts with those who will receive the message.

One day Jesus stopped at a well where some woman drew some water. It was here that Jesus met the Samaritan woman. Her life was forever changed by this encounter with Jesus. When Philip was commissioned to go to a certain road, he went, and that is where he found the Eunuch reading the Word of God. Being prompted by the Holy Spirit He went and opened the Word of God to the Eunuch. The Eunuch's life was forever changed because of that encounter and sharing the Word of God.

There are many examples in the Bible. For us it is important to go, under the direction of the Holy Spirit and share the Word God places in our hearts. The Discipleship journey starts with us leading people to accept Jesus as Lord over their lives.

How to Evangelise?

This answer is explored in detail in the designated chapter on "Sharing your Faith." There are many, and effective, ways to share your faith. We know of the Evangelism Explosion Strategy, the Four Spiritual Laws, The John 3 verse 16 gospel presentation, Service Evangelism, Prayer Evangelism and many more. Your circumstance will determine which one is the most effective to be a witness for Jesus.

The most effective and efficient strategy of evangelism is a changed and transformed life!

We are called and anointed to be witnesses. The best and by far the most effective witness and testimony we can carry in our lives is a changed life.

Step 2 – Finding "Worthy" Disciples

Step 2 is to start making disciples of these converts. The quality of Disciples we make will determine the impact their lives will have on others around them.

The extent to which you will be able to make Disciples is the extent to which your church will grow in a healthy way. Disciples are those men and woman where your Peace will find rest in their hearts. You know that you have found a Disciple if they, out of their own free will, express a desire that you help them grow in their faith, however, even then, be wise in who you Disciple. Build the strongest team that you are able to lead for the Lord Jesus.

1. Jesus' strategy for finding "Worthy" men and woman.

When Jesus sent out His Disciples to go and preach the Gospel, He gave them a wonderful strategy. I believe this strategy will serve you well in planting dynamic Churches.

> Matthew 10:11-13 (NIV) "11Whatever town or village you enter, search there for some worthy person and stay at their house until you leave. 12 As you enter the home, give it your greeting. 13 If the home is deserving, let your peace rest on it; if it is not, let your peace return to you."

Finding a Worthy man, in the town, suburb or place where God calls you to go and plant a Church, is essential. Always look for people who could and would take the message you bring to them, further.

A Worthy man is defined by being a man of worth. Worthy people are visionary. They are the people who love to be involved with people who have a vision. The only vision poor people have, is what you have on offer for them, whereas worthy people, will help you fulfill the vision God gave you. If you share a vision with worthy people, they will frequently ask and offer their help to see that vision fulfilled. Worthy people are people who take action and take responsibility. You would be wise to ask God for "Worthy" men and woman to start your new ministry with.

A "***worthy man***" could be a man or a woman or a couple. A worthy man is someone who runs his or her own business, small or large, or manages or leads a business, organisation or industry. A worthy man could be the principle or department head of a School, College or Educational institution. The worthy man is distinguished by their stand, reputation and stature in the community.

The example of the Lord..............................

All of this came from the pattern and model Jesus gave when He started His ministry on earth with worthy men. Even though Jesus declared in Luke 4 that the "Spirit of the Lord is upon me to preach the Good News to the Poor" He never started His ministry with poor people. He started His ministry with "Worthy men."

Luke tells us that He first went past the Tax booth of Levi and called him to follow Him.

> Luke 5:27-28 (NIV) "27 After this, Jesus went out and saw a tax collector by the name of Levi sitting at his tax booth. "Follow me," Jesus said to him, 28 and Levi got up, left everything and followed him."

Levi was a "***Worthy man***." In those days the Tax Collectors were like the wealthiest people around. They were like Bankers who rolled in the money.

Then we see Jesus was walking by the sea of Galilee and He got into the boat belonging to Simon Peter. Peter was not just a Fisherman, no, he was the owner of a fishing boat, and if we read the whole portion we see that he had a crew, and so did his partners, James and John.

> Luke 5:3 (NIV) "3 He got into one of the boats, **the one belonging to Simon**, and asked him to put out a little from shore. Then he sat down and taught the people from the boat."

> Luke 5:9-11 (NIV) "9 For he and all his companions were astonished at the catch of fish they had taken, 10 and

> so were James and John, the sons of Zebedee, Simon's partners. Then Jesus said to Simon, "Don't be afraid; from now on you will fish for people." 11 So **they pulled their boats up on shore, left everything and followed him.**"

We know from Colossians 4 verse 14 that Luke was a doctor. We can see that these disciples were worthy men since they were Fishermen, a Tax Collector and a Doctor. We also know that Judas handled the money, hence we could assume that he was a worthy man as well who could be trusted with the Lord's finances.

2. The example of the Apostle Paul's Church Planting ministry.

The Apostle Paul, when he planted the church in Philippi, found this principle in operation. You will recall that he had this "Macedonian Call" and straightaway went to the region of Macedonia to preach the Word of God there. Acts 16 verses 12-15 tell us this amazing affirmative story of this principle being applied. It was there that he immediately met a "Worthy Woman" called Lydia. She invited them to her house, where they stayed until the church was established.

Another example came from when Paul planted the church in Corinth. He met a "***Worthy Man and Woman***." Priscilla and Aquila were a.............................. like him. Once he found this "Worthy Man" he stayed with them and from there the Church grew.

> Acts 18:1-3 (NIV) "[18:1] After this, Paul left Athens and went to Corinth. [2] There he met a Jew named Aquila, a native of Pontus, who had recently come from Italy with his wife Priscilla, because Claudius had ordered all the Jews to leave Rome. Paul went to see them, [3] and because he was a tentmaker as they were, he stayed and worked with them."

3. The Teaching of the Apostle Paul to his Disciple.

Interestingly, and most noteworthy for us is the fact that the Apostle Paul gave this same advice to his disciple, and spiritual son, Timothy. In 2 Timothy 2 verse 2 we read that he advised Timothy to "***entrust to reliable people***" the things he learnt and observed from Paul. He advised him to entrust these truths to people "***who will also be qualified to teach others.***"

> 2 Timothy 2:2 (NIV) 2 And the things you have heard me say in the presence of many witnesses entrust to reliable people who will also be qualified to teach others.

One of the essentials to planting dynamic churches is starting with the right people. Worthy and reliable people need to be your first disciples.

Where do we find these Disciples?

Finding disciples could be found in two primary areas:

1. They could be those whom God gives you right from the start from within your current Church, such as was the situation with the Apostles Paul and Barnabas in the Church in Antioch when the Holy Spirit called them to go out on their first Missionary journey. We read this amazing story in Acts 13 verses 1-5.
2. These disciples could be found by sharing the Gospel among those who come to the Lord through the preaching of the Word such as what we find in Acts 19 verses 1-12.

Fast and pray before you search for Disciples.

This process of finding and choosing disciples always starts with a season of Fasting and Prayer. Jesus spent a night praying before He chose His Disciples. God chose Paul and Barnabas during a time of Fasting and Prayer in the church in Antioch. The process of finding your disciples to disciple might take you three to nine months.

> Matthew 28:19 (NIV)" [19] Therefore go and make disciples of all nations, baptizing them in the name of the Father and of the Son and of the Holy Spirit,"

As you go, seek and save the Lost, and teach them to observe everything the Lord taught you.

Step 3 is to Disciple the "Worthy" men.

Finding Disciples is one thing, but "teaching them to observe" is another. Jesus called us to teach our Disciples the very things He taught His Disciples. Remember, the early Church never had the New Testament like we have it today. They had the Apostles teaching them and their teachings became known as the "Apostles Teachings." The "Apostles Teachings" was really just Jesus' Teachings, which they conveyed and taught the New Believers.

Discipleship is the intentionally process of teaching someone the teachings of Jesus. Developing a clearly defined process of Discipleship is essential to fulfilling the Great Commission.

> Matthew 28:20 NIV "20 and teaching them to obey everything I have commanded you. And surely I am with you always, to the very end of the age."

There are basically Five Steps in the Process of Discipleship.

1. **Salvation**. The stage of leading someone to an enduring encounter with Jesus Christ. It is the phase of leading them to make a firm decision to make Jesus the Lord of their lives, solidify that decision through Baptism and laying a strong foundation for their faith.

2. **Establishing Roots, Values and Spiritual Disciplines.** During this stage we teach our Disciples to observe the Values of the Kingdom, while establishing spiritual Disciplines. These Values and Spiritual Disciplines become the Spiritual Roots of our Faith.
3. **Developing Gifts and Skills.** During this Phase we help our Disciples to discover the Gifts of God upon their lives. We help them develop their Gifts and Skills to fulfil the purpose of God upon their lives. This is an equipping phase.
4. **Being Fruitful.** The key to a process of Discipleship is putting Gifts and Skills into practice. Being Fruitful also deals with us living a life worth following. Winning Souls is bearing fruit. Being Fruitful is helping your Disciples to effectively equip their Disciples through the Process of Discipleship.
5. **Multiplication.** Our Disciples making and launching their Disciples into their purpose mark this phase.

Step 4. Gather "Worthy men" in groups.

One of the strategies we learnt from Jesus through the way He discipled His Disciples was that He discipled them in a group. Rarely do we see Him doing one on one discipling. He sometimes discipled two or three separately, however, most of the time He discipled them all together.

We read in Matthew 5 when Jesus started discipling His Disciples. He started by calling them together and then He taught them in a group. One of the successes I've seen around the world of effective discipleship is that it happens in groups.

- **Timewise.** In a time where we need to be wise with our time, it maximises our time to equip our disciples by doing it in a group.
- **Accountability.** Learning in groups provide for an opportunity to be accountable, not just to the Leader, but also to one another.

- **Collaboration.** Learn from one another, and to work together as a team. When Jesus sent His disciples out to put into practice what He taught them, He sent them out two by two.

7

THE PROCESS OF DISCIPLESHIP

We all agree that the "Great Commission" is for each one of us to "Go, and make disciples of all nations," however; very few of us have a clearly defined plan or process of "How" we do that, or "What" we need to do it.

Following is one example, for making disciples like Jesus did:

Step One – Salvation.

The first step in the Process of Discipleship is to make sure that people are "Born again." The Discipleship journey will only bear fruit if it is built on the Foundation of Salvation.

Salvation is a two-part Miracle

To be "SAVED" is the process of being "Born Again," to become a "Child of God."

To be "Saved" is to be "Converted."

From a human perspective, this process of becoming a Child of God is called:

.................................," and is the voluntary change in the mind of a sinner, on one the one hand, from sin, and on the other hand, to Christ. This human perspective is not the result of human initiation, but a mere response to the work of the Holy Spirit inside of us. The turning from our sin is called................................., and the turning to Christ is called ....

To be "Saved" is to be "Regenerated."

From a Godly perspective, this process is called "..," and is the act of God whereby God makes us new creations, creates in us a new heart and puts a new spirit within us. God removing our sin, the wall of separation removed between Him and us, and Him making us holy and pure as He is, declaring us righteous, further extends this act of God. This is when we are "born again."

Elementary Principles

Phase One explores the essentials to allow the incorruptible Seed of God's Word to take root in our lives so that we can believe and be saved. The writer to the Hebrews outlines the six foundational principles in following Christ.

> Hebrews 6:1-2 (NKJV) "1 Therefore, leaving the discussion of **the elementary principles of Christ**, let us go on to perfection, not laying again the foundation of repentance from dead works and of faith toward God, 2 of the doctrine of baptisms, of laying on of hands, of resurrection of the dead, and of eternal judgment."

Within these two verses we find the ***elementary principles*** of life in Christ. They are ***1. Repentance from dead works, 2. Faith towards God,***

3. Baptisms, 4. Laying on of Hands, 5. Resurrection of the dead, and 6. Eternal judgment. If we build our relationship upon these elementary principles and add to them spiritual disciplines and the development of good and sound spiritual roots, it will set us up for tremendous growth and we will see the Seed of God produce in us fruitfulness.

These six foundations were installed and taught to every New Believer. Laying a solid and sound foundation to build one's faith on is essential to build a spiritual house that will withstand the storms of life.

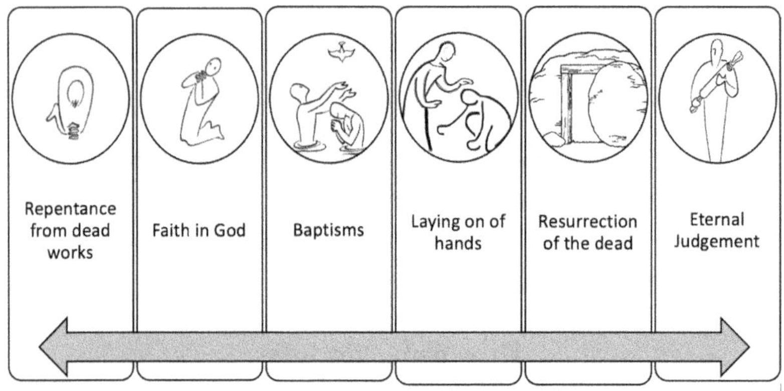

Salvation Overview Diagram

a. Repentance from dead works.

The ***departure point,*** in following Christ, should be "..................................."from dead works. Many think that they can come closer to God by doing good works, but there is only one way to come close to God and that is through Faith in Jesus Christ.

Repentance marks "our part" in responding to the work of the Holy Spirit inside of us. Sin .... us from God.

> Isaiah 59:2 (NKJV) "2 But your iniquities have separated you from your God; And your sins have hidden His face from you, So that He will not hear."

.... sinned.

The Bible says that: "All have sinned and fall short of the Glory of God." All of us sinned and are in need of forgiveness of our sins.

> Romans 3:23 (NIV) "23 for all have sinned and fall short of the glory of God,"

What will redeem us from our sin?

The only redeeming price for sin is the .... of Jesus.

> 1 Peter 1:18-19 (NKJV) "18 knowing that you were not redeemed with corruptible things, like silver or gold, from your aimless conduct received by tradition from your fathers, 19 but with the precious blood of Christ, as of a lamb without blemish and without spot."

We need a Saviour!

Christ is our .... Only He can take our sins away. Only He made a way to take away our sins and to bring us into a restored relationship with the Father.

> Luke 2:11 (NKJV) "11 For there is born to you this day in the city of David a Saviour, who is Christ the Lord."

> Matthew 1:21 (NKJV) "21 And she will bring forth a Son, and you shall call His name Jesus, for He will save His people from their sins."

How can I be saved from my sins?
I need to repent from my sins.

On the day of Pentecost, Peter stood up and boldly preached a message, calling everyone to "repent, be baptised and to wait for the gift of the Holy Spirit."

> Acts 2:37-38 (NKJV) "37 Now when they heard this, they were cut to the heart, and said to Peter and the rest of the apostles, "Men and brethren, what shall we do?" 38 Then Peter said to them, "Repent, and let every one of you be baptized in the name of Jesus Christ for the remission of sins; and you shall receive the gift of the Holy Spirit."

What does it mean to "Repent?"

Repentance means that you make a roundabout turn in your .... and .... Repentance is to change your mind and actions to conformity to the Will and purpose of God.

What we see here is that:

> *"Repentance is a place we come to in our lives where we look at our lives with ...., reflect over our actions with ...., and then turn .... from our sins, ... our course, our views and .... the Will of God, over ours."*

The way we give expression to this "change of heart and mind" is that we express true sorrow for our actions, behaviour and sins, and then confess our sins.

> 2 Corinthians 7:9-11 (NKJV) "9 Now I rejoice, not that you were made sorry, but that your sorrow led to repentance. For you were made sorry in a godly manner, that you might suffer loss from us in nothing. 10 For godly sorrow produces repentance leading to salvation, not to be regretted; but the sorrow of the world produces death. 11 For observe this very thing, that you sorrowed in a godly manner: What diligence it produced in you, what clearing of yourselves, what indignation, what fear, what vehement desire, what zeal, what vindication! In all

things you proved yourselves to be clear in this matter."

Hence, we could say that repentance means more than being sorry for what has been done, although .... always accompanies true repentance. Repentance also means that we stop sinning, deliberately. True sorrow will lead to repentance and that will lead you to salvation.

How do we "Repent?"

- **We Repent when we accept the Holy Spirit's .... inside of us.**

The Bible says that the Holy Spirit is now that active agent working inside of us to help us come to a place of repentance. The Holy Spirit convicts us of sin.

John 16:8-11 (NKJV) "8 And when He (Holy Spirit) has come, He will convict the world of sin, and of righteousness, and of judgment: 9 of sin, because they do not believe in Me; 10 of righteousness, because I go to My Father and you see Me no more; 11 of judgment, because the ruler of this world is judged."

- **We come to repentance when we .... to God and stop hardening our ....**

Hebrews 4:7 (NKJV) "Today, if you will hear His voice, Do not harden your hearts."

- **We come to repentance when we make confession of our ....**

We have this assurance that when we confess our sins that He will forgive us our sins and cleanse us.

> 1 John 1:9 (NKJV) "9 If we confess our sins, He is faithful and just to forgive us our sins and to cleanse us from all unrighteousness."

b. Faith in God.

The ***second part of being born again*** is to "***put your faith in God.***" Jesus, spoke to Nicodemus and explained to him that he needed to be 'Born again' to enter into the Kingdom of God. Unless a person repents, places their faith in God, and accepts Christ as their Lord and Saviour, no conversion or regeneration can take place. This conversion experience is described by Christ as being " ...." Being "***Born Again***" marks the beginning of our discipleship journey.

> John 3:3-5 (NKJV) "3 Jesus answered and said to him, "Most assuredly, I say to you, unless one is born again, he cannot see the kingdom of God." 4 Nicodemus said to Him, "How can a man be born when he is old? Can he enter a second time into his mother's womb and be born?" 5 Jesus answered, "Most assuredly, I say to you, unless one is born of water and the Spirit, he cannot enter the kingdom of God."

To be 'Born again" requires of us to ".................................. "of our sins, ...to the conviction of the Holy Spirit inside of us, AND, put our .... in Jesus Christ.

How do I put my faith in Jesus Christ?

The definition for "Faith" is:

"Faith is confidence or trust in .... or thing; or the observance of an obligation from ....; or fidelity to a ...., promise and engagement.

What do we believe, to be true, so that we could have faith in Jesus?

1. We believe that Jesus is the .... of God.

The first place we need to look at, in putting our faith in God, is .... we put our faith in. Jesus is at the centre of this journey.

> Matthew 1:23 (NKJV) "23 "Behold, the virgin shall be with child, and bear a Son, and they shall call His name Immanuel," which is translated, "God with us.""

> Matthew 3:17 (NKJV) "17 And suddenly a voice came from heaven, saying, "This is My beloved ...., *in whom I am well pleased."*

Jesus once asked His Disciples who people say that He was. The Apostle Peter stated, and it is recorded in Matthew, that He is "the Christ, the Son of the Living God."

> Matthew 16:15-16 (NKJV) "15 He said to them, "But who do you say that I am?" 16 Simon Peter answered and said, "You are the Christ, the Son of the living God.""

> Matthew 26:63-64 (NKJV) "63 But Jesus kept silent. And the high priest answered and said to Him, "I put You under oath by the living God: Tell us if You are the Christ, the Son of God!" 64 Jesus said to him, "It is as you said. Nevertheless, I say to you, hereafter you will see the Son of Man sitting at the right hand of the Power, and coming on the clouds of heaven.""

2. We believe that He .... on the Cross of Calvary for our sins.

What did Jesus do on earth?

Matthew 1:21 (NKJV) "21 And she will bring forth a Son, and you shall call His name Jesus, for He will save His people from their sins.""

The Apostle John reports that God sent His Son to die for us.

John 3:16 (NKJV) "16 For God so loved the world that He gave His only begotten Son, that whoever believes in Him should .... but have everlasting life."

3. We believe that He .... from the dead and is .... and seated on the .... hand of God the Father.

Before Jesus died on the cross, He declared to His Disciples that He would rise from the dead.

Romans 14:9 (NKJV) "9 For to this end Christ died and rose and lived again, that He might be Lord of both the dead and the living."

4.We believe that .... for our .... is found only in Jesus Christ.

Only in Jesus Christ do we find such forgiveness from sins. Putting our faith in Jesus, is believing that He forgives us of all our sins and redeems us through His blood.

Ephesians 1:7 (NIV) [7] In him we have redemption through his blood, the forgiveness of sins, in accordance with the riches of God's grace."

Acts 13:38 (NIV) [38] "Therefore, my brothers, I want you to know that through Jesus the forgiveness of sins is proclaimed to you."

5. We ....when we, place our .... in Jesus to be our Lord and Saviour.

Believing in Jesus requires us to get into the wheelbarrow and trust Jesus with our whole lives.

> Acts 16:30-31, 33b, 34c (NKJV) "30 And he brought them
> out and said, "Sirs, what must I do to be saved?" 31
> So they said, "Believe on the Lord Jesus Christ, and
> you will be saved, you and your household.""33 ...
> And immediately he and all his family were baptized.
> 34...; and he rejoiced, having believed in God with all
> his household."

The Jailer asked the question that we are exploring right now: "***What must I do to be saved?***"

The answer came immediately: ".................................. on the Lord Jesus Christ, and you will be saved."

That message is still the same today: "***Believe on the Lord Jesus Christ, and you will be saved.***"

> Romans 10:9 (NKJV) "9 that if you ……...............................
> with your mouth the Lord Jesus and ……………… in
> your heart that God has raised Him from the dead,
> you will be ...."

Maybe you've never confessed with your mouth that Jesus Christ is your Lord. Take this opportunity to say to the Lord Jesus: "***Jesus Christ, I want you to be the Lord over my life. Jesus Christ, I believe in you.***"

c. The Doctrine of Baptisms.

The ***third part of Step One***, of establishing the ***elementary foundations of Salvation***, deals with the importance of "***Baptisms***."

• • •

The Doctrine of Baptisms consists of, ***Baptism into the Body of Christ***, the ***Baptism of Believers*** and the ***Baptism in the Holy Spirit***. We have a number of Biblical examples to emphasise this progression from Regeneration - Baptism into the Body of Christ, to Baptism in water, to receiving the Baptism of the Holy Spirit.

> Hebrews 6:1-2 (NKJV) "1 Therefore, leaving the discussion of the elementary principles of Christ, let us go on to perfection, not laying again the foundation of repentance from dead works and of faith toward God, 2 of the doctrine of baptisms, of laying on of hands, of resurrection of the dead, and of eternal judgment."

- **Baptism into the Body of Christ.**

In one sense we already discussed the first Baptism into the Body of Christ in our previous sessions, when we discussed about being "Born again." This is a work of God through the Holy Spirit at regeneration.

> 1 Corinthians 12:13 (NIV 1984) 13 For we were all baptized by one Spirit into one body–whether Jews or Greeks, slave or free–and we were all given the one Spirit to drink."

- **The Baptism of Believers.**

Jesus emphasised that .... should be baptised, as a necessary step after believing.

> Mark 16:16 (NIV) [16] Whoever believes and is baptized will be saved, but whoever does not believe will be condemned.

- **Baptism of the Holy Spirit.**

Towards the end of Jesus' ministry, He emphasised to His Disciples the importance of water baptism and the subsequent Baptism with the Holy Spirit.

> Acts 1:5 (NIV) [5] For John baptized with water, but in a few days you will be baptized with the Holy Spirit."

The Apostles preached the Gospel, and then immediately after people responded to the message, emphasised that these new believers should be baptised, and they received the Holy Spirit.

> Acts 2:37-38 (NKJV) "37 Now when they heard this, they were cut to the heart, and said to Peter and the rest of the apostles, "Men and brethren, what shall we do?" 38 Then Peter said to them, "Repent, and let every one of you be baptized in the name of Jesus Christ for the remission of sins; and you shall receive the gift of the Holy Spirit."

The Apostles were quite intentional in their pursuit of new believers being baptised.

> Acts 8:14-17 (NIV) '[14] When the apostles in Jerusalem heard that Samaria had accepted the word of God, they sent Peter and John to them. [15] When they arrived, they prayed for them that they might receive the Holy Spirit, [16] because the Holy Spirit had not yet come upon any of them; they had simply been baptized into the name of the Lord Jesus. [17] Then Peter and John placed their hands on them, and they received the Holy Spirit."

> Acts 19:4-7 (NIV) [4] Paul said, "John's baptism was a baptism of repentance. He told the people to believe

> in the one coming after him, that is, in Jesus." [5] On hearing this, they were baptized into the name of the Lord Jesus. [6] When Paul placed his hands on them, the Holy Spirit came on them, and they spoke in tongues and prophesied. [7] There were about twelve men in all.

In these few verses, among many New Testament examples, we find examples of an order of how the Apostles discipled. We clearly see the ***progression*** from ***conversion/regeneration***, to ***baptism in water***, to ***baptism in the Holy Spirit***. These three basic initial elements of the Discipleship journey are essential starting blocks. We see that the disciples were intentional, to preach the Gospel, and then ensure that these new believers were Baptised, and then let them receive the Holy Spirit.

Let us take a few moments and look at the Baptism of Believers:

Method of Baptism.

The Biblical method of Baptism is by immersion. The Greek Word for Baptise is the word "Baptismo" which means to ....

Who can be Baptised?

Believers can be Baptised, and in fact, should be baptised, for reasons to be explained next. Hence it is called the Baptism of Believers.

Baptism is for ....

Since the instruction is clear from Scripture that those who believe should be Baptised, we call it the "Baptism of Believers."

> Mark 16:15-16 (NKJV) "15 And He said to them, "Go into all the world and preach the gospel to every creature.

> 16 He who believes and is baptized will be saved; but he who does not believe will be condemned."

What happens when we are baptised?

Through Baptism we .... our old selves and .... to a new life.

Baptism is an ordinance of the Church, not as some ritualistic man-made requirement, but as one ordained by God. Let us take a moment and take a deeper look at the Baptism of Believers. Romans 6 summarises these two concepts beautifully.

> Romans 6:3-4 (NIV) "[3] Or don't you know that all of us who were baptized into Christ Jesus were baptized into his death? [4] We were therefore buried with him through baptism into death in order that, just as Christ was raised from the dead through the glory of the Father, we too may live a new life."

> Galatians 3:27 (NIV) "[27] for all of you who were baptized into Christ have clothed yourselves with Christ."

Symbolism of Baptism explained:

Firstly, Into the water, speaks of .... unto self.

Secondly, out of the water, speaks of .... to a new life, and .... oneself with Christ.

The Baptism of the Holy Spirit.

This part on the session on Baptism is equally important, and that involves the baptism with the Holy Spirit. When the Apostles heard that Samaria received the Word of the Lord, they went over to pray for them that they might receive the Holy Spirit.

> Acts 8:12 (NKJV) "12 But when they believed Philip as he preached the things concerning the kingdom of God and the name of Jesus Christ, both men and women were baptized."

> Acts 8:14-17 (NIV) '[14] When the apostles in Jerusalem heard that Samaria had accepted the word of God, they sent Peter and John to them. [15] When they arrived, they prayed for them that they might receive the Holy Spirit, [16] because the Holy Spirit had not yet come upon any of them; they had simply been baptized into the name of the Lord Jesus. [17] Then Peter and John placed their hands on them, and they received the Holy Spirit."

Why is the Baptism of the Holy Spirit important for Believers?

The ***Baptism of the Holy Spirit*** is important, since ***it was a Promise of something Jesus would bring***.

Ever since the time John, the Baptist, started his ministry, he pointed to One that would come after him and would "***Baptise with the Holy Spirit.***" It seems from John's message that the real baptism they should seek is that of being Baptised with the Holy Spirit.

> Matthew 3:11 "11 I indeed baptize you with water unto repentance, but He who is coming after me is mightier than I, whose sandals I am not worthy to carry. He will baptize you with the Holy Spirit and fire."

We see that Jesus confirmed and continued to encourage His Disciples to wait for this Gift of the Holy Spirit in Acts 1 verses 4 to 5. ***What***

was this "Promise of the Father?" It was the ***"Baptism with the Holy Spirit."***

> Acts 1:4-5 (NKJV) "4 And being assembled together with them, He commanded them not to depart from Jerusalem, but to wait for the Promise of the Father, "which," He said, "you have heard from Me; 5 for John truly baptized with water, but you shall be baptized with the Holy Spirit not many days from now."

We also see that Jesus promised that ***they would receive "power"*** when they ***would receive the Holy Spirit***, and that they ***would be "His witnesses."***

> Acts 1:8 (NKJV) "8 But you shall receive power when the Holy Spirit has come upon you; and you shall be witnesses to Me in Jerusalem, and in all Judea and Samaria, and to the end of the earth."

We see in Acts chapter 2 verse 4 that ***they received the Baptism with the Holy Spirit.***

> Acts 2:4 (NKJV) "4 And they were all filled with the Holy Spirit and began to speak with other tongues, as the Spirit gave them utterance."

The Apostles made sure that everyone who were ***"Born again" received the Holy Spirit.***

> Acts 8:14-17 14 Now when the apostles who were at Jerusalem heard that Samaria had received the word of God, they sent Peter and John to them, 15 who, when they had come down, prayed for them that they might receive the Holy Spirit. 16 For as yet He had

fallen upon none of them.They had only been baptized in the name of the Lord Jesus. 17 Then they laid hands on them, and they received the Holy Spirit."

This was also the practice of the Apostle Paul.

Acts 19:1-6 (NKJV) "1 And it happened, while Apollos was at Corinth, that Paul, having passed through the upper regions, came to Ephesus. And finding some disciples 2 he said to them, "Did you receive the Holy Spirit when you believed?" So they said to him, "We have not so much as heard whether there is a Holy Spirit." 3 And he said to them, "Into what then were you baptized?" So they said, "Into John's baptism." 4 Then Paul said, "John indeed baptized with a baptism of repentance, saying to the people that they should believe on Him who would come after him, that is, on Christ Jesus." 5 When they heard this, they were baptized in the name of the Lord Jesus. 6 And when Paul had laid hands on them, the Holy Spirit came upon them, and they spoke with tongues and prophesied."

What happens when I receive the baptism of the Holy Spirit?

Evidence of the Holy Spirit's Baptism.

New Testament examples

In the New Testament, we have a number of examples of when Believers received the Baptism of the Holy Spirit. In the book of Acts, the most common sign of Holy Spirit baptism was the speaking in unknown tongues. In Jesus' final instructions to His Disciples, He described to them the signs that will follow those who put their faith in Him. One of the signs was that "they will speak with new tongues."

> Mark 16:17(NKJV) "17 And these signs will follow those who believe: In My name they will cast out demons; they will speak with new tongues;"

So, it was no surprise to them that when they were all baptized in the Holy Spirit that they all spoke in other tongues.

In fact, of the five accounts we have in the Book of Acts, three explicitly describe the evidence of tongues, and other example, that of the Apostle Paul, by later revealed Scriptural knowledge, also spoke in tongues. Only one occasion does not make that distinction. Let's look at these occurrences.

1. The Apostles.

On the day of Pentecost, whilst they were all together in one accord, the Holy Spirit came upon all of them and baptised them all and they all spoke in other tongues as the Spirit gave them utterance.

> Acts 2:4 (NKJV) "4 And they were all filled with the Holy Spirit and began to speak with other tongues, as the Spirit gave them utterance."

2. New Believers in Samaria.

In Acts chapter 8 we read that the people in Samaria received the Word of God and were baptised in the Name of Jesus. The Apostles sent Peter and John from Jerusalem to these Believers to enquire whether they received the Baptism of the Holy Spirit.

> Acts 8:14-17 (NIV) "[14] When the apostles in Jerusalem heard that Samaria had accepted the word of God, they sent Peter and John to them. [15] When they arrived, they prayed for them that they might receive the Holy Spirit, [16] because the Holy Spirit had not yet come upon any of them; they had simply been baptised into the name of the Lord Jesus. [17] Then

> Peter and John placed their hands on them, and they received the Holy Spirit."

3. Saul of Tarsus (Apostle Paul)

In Acts 9 we read of how God sent Ananias to a certain street in Damascus to lay his hands on him to receive back his eye sight and to receive the in filling of the Holy Spirit.

> Acts 9:17-18 (NKJV) "17 And Ananias went his way and entered the house; and laying his hands on him he said, "Brother Saul, the Lord Jesus, who appeared to you on the road as you came, has sent me that you may receive your sight and be filled with the Holy Spirit." 18 Immediately there fell from his eyes something like scales, and he received his sight at once; and he arose and was baptized."

On this specific account there is no mention of him speaking in other tongues. However, when we look at what the Apostle write about in his letter to the church in Corinth, he confirms that He speaks in tongue, which allows one to draw the obvious conclusion that whether it is mentioned or not, there is an association between the Baptism of the Holy Spirit and speaking in tongues.

> 1 Corinthians 14:18 (NKJV) "18 I thank my God I speak with tongues more than you all;"

So, even though it did not specifically mention that Paul Spoke in tongues when he received the Baptism with the Holy Spirit, He nevertheless did.

4. Cornelius and His Household.

When God called Peter to go to the household of Cornelius, he did not expect these uncircumcised people to accept the Word of God and neither that they would be baptised in the Holy Spirit in the manner they did. While he was still speaking, the Holy Spirit baptised these Believers and they all spoke in tongues. How did the Apostles know that Cornelius and his household were baptised in the Holy Spirit? They heard them speaking in other tongues, just as they did when they received the Holy Spirit.

> Acts 10:44-48 (NIV) [44] While Peter was still speaking these words, the Holy Spirit came on all who heard the message. [45] The circumcised believers who had come with Peter were astonished that the gift of the Holy Spirit had been poured out even on the Gentiles. [46] For they heard them speaking in tongues and praising God. Then Peter said, [47] "Can anyone keep these people from being baptised with water? They have received the Holy Spirit just as we have." [48] So he ordered that they be baptised in the name of Jesus Christ. Then they asked Peter to stay with them for a few days."

This is an amazing account of gentiles receiving the Word of God and being filled with the Holy Spirit.

5. Disciples at Ephesus.

The last account we read of in the Book of Acts is that from when the Apostle Paul went to Ephesus. Once again we have an account of people believing, without being baptised, and without receiving the Holy Spirit's Baptism at conversion. However, subsequent to some teaching, they were baptised in the Name of the Lord Jesus (Believers Baptism) and after Paul laid his hands on them, they received the baptism of the Holy Spirit.

> Acts 19:1-7 (NIV) Paul in Ephesus [19:1] While Apollos was at Corinth, Paul took the road through the interior and arrived at Ephesus. There he found some

> disciples [2] and asked them, "Did you receive the Holy Spirit when you believed?" They answered, "No, we have not even heard that there is a Holy Spirit."
>
> So Paul asked, "Then what baptism did you receive?" "John's baptism," they replied. [4] Paul said, "John's baptism was a baptism of repentance. He told the people to believe in the one coming after him, that is, in Jesus." [5] On hearing this, they were baptised into the name of the Lord Jesus. [6] When Paul placed his hands on them, the Holy Spirit came on them, and they spoke in tongues and prophesied. [7] There were about twelve men in all.

Even though we've looked at these Scriptural examples, the apostle Paul says that not all will speak in tongues.

> I Corinthians 12:30 "Are all apostles? Are all prophets? Are all teachers? Are all workers of miracles? Have all the gifts of healing? do all speak with tongues? do all interpret?"

How can I receive the Baptism with the Holy Spirit?

1. Ask the Lord to baptise you with the Holy Spirit.

The first thing I encourage you to do is to ask the Father for His Holy Spirit. He promised the Holy Spirit to us as Believers. Believe and receive His promise!

> Luke 11:13 (NKJV) "13 If you then, being evil, know how to give good gifts to your children, how much more will your heavenly Father give the Holy Spirit to those who ask Him!""

2. Drink from the fountain of Living waters.

The second thing I encourage you to do is to present yourself before God with an expectation, hungry and thirsty for the Living Water of His Spirit. Jesus, on one occasion, spoke about the Holy Spirit, and compared His presence within us to that of having a spring of Living water inside of us.

> John 7:37-39 (NKJV) "37 On the last day, that great day of the feast, Jesus stood and cried out, saying, "If anyone thirsts, let him come to Me and drink. 38 He who believes in Me, as the Scripture has said, out of his heart will flow rivers of living water." 39 But this He spoke concerning the Spirit, whom those believing in Him would receive; for the Holy Spirit was not yet given, because Jesus was not yet glorified."

3. Receive the Baptism of the Holy Spirit through the laying on of hands.

On a number of occasions we read, in the Book of Acts, that Believers received the Baptism of the Holy Spirit through the Laying on of hands.

> Acts 8:17(NKJV) "17 Then they laid hands on them, and they received the Holy Spirit."

> Acts 19:6 (NKJV) "6 And when Paul had laid hands on them, the Holy Spirit came upon them, and they spoke with tongues and prophesied."

4. Receive the Baptism of the Holy Spirit while worshipping and praying.

Prayer and Worship are two of the most powerful atmosphere settings you could position yourself in to receive the Baptism of the Holy Spirit.

On the Day of Pentecost, the Disciples were together, "in one accord," and while they were in this place of spiritual unity, possibly praying, they received the Baptism of the Holy Spirit.

> Acts 2:1 (NKJV) "1 When the Day of Pentecost had fully come, they were all with one accord in one place."

> Acts 2:2 (NKJV) "2 And suddenly there came a sound from heaven, as of a rushing mighty wind, and it filled the whole house where they were sitting."

What will happen to you?

1. You might start to speak in tongues.
2. You might be overcome with emotion as the Holy Spirit fills you. It is not an emotion of sadness, but one of joy and amazement.
3. You might start to boldly prophecy, by speaking the Word of God over people's lives, uncharacteristic to how you would normally behave.
4. You might start to sing a new song of praise and exultation to the Lord. It will not bother you since it will be like something has come over you and it will just well up from within you. You will truly experience the spring of living water welling up from within.
5. You might experience exceeding joy and gladness as you as submersed, in a sense, in the Power of the Holy Spirit.

I pray that you will share this wonderful promise of the Father.

d. Laying on of Hands.

The Laying on of hands is that ministry that takes places where God touches others, through His commissioned servants, to commission certain people for specific divine purposes, to make conciliation, to bring healing to the sick, and to bestow gifts, especially the Gift of the Holy Spirit.

Throughout the Old Testament we see that the laying on of .... was practiced in the commissioning of people for divine .... and purposes.

On all occasions the laying on of hands came from a .... instruction from the Lord, and it should therefor always be upheld and honoured as such as we practice this in the Church.

> Numbers 27:18-20 (NKJV) "18 And the Lord said to Moses: "Take Joshua the son of Nun with you, a man in whom is the Spirit, and lay your.................................. on him; 19 set him before Eleazar the priest and before all the congregation, and inaugurate him in their sight. 20 And you shall give some of your .... to him, that all the congregation of the children of Israel may be obedient."

> Numbers 27:23 (NKJV) "23 And he laid his .... on him and inaugurated him, just as the .... commanded by the hand of Moses."

> Deuteronomy 34:9 (NKJV) "9 Now Joshua the son of Nun was full of the spirit of ...., for Moses had laid his .... on him; so the children of Israel heeded him, and did as the Lord had commanded Moses."

This is a Holy Ordinance which should be done 1. Under the direct instruction of the Lord, and 2. In the presence of all the congregation, who will 3. Willingly adhered to their instructions as unto the Lord.

> Acts 6:3-6 (NKJV) "3 Therefore, brethren, seek out from among you seven men of good reputation, full of the Holy Spirit and wisdom, whom we may appoint over

this business; 4 but we will give ourselves continually to prayer and to the ministry of the word."

5 And the saying pleased the whole multitude. And they chose Stephen, a man full of faith and the Holy Spirit, and Philip, Prochorus, Nicanor, Timon, Parmenas, and Nicolas, a proselyte from Antioch, 6 whom they set before the apostles; and when they had prayed, they laid hands on them."

Acts 13:3 (NKJV) "1 Now in the church that was at Antioch there were certain prophets and teachers: Barnabas, Simeon who was called Niger, Lucius of Cyrene, Manaen who had been brought up with Herod the tetrarch, and Saul. 2 As they ministered to the Lord and fasted, the Holy Spirit said, "Now separate to Me Barnabas and Saul for the work to which I have called them." 3 Then, having fasted and prayed, and laid hands on them, they sent them away."

It is this "***laying on of hands***" that was honoured and regarded in the early church, both by the people who were "***commissioned***" and "***anointed***" for their "***higher calling***" and service, and by those who observed the '***Laying on of Hands.***". These men and woman were held in high regard, since the Lord set them apart by the "***laying on of hands***" for their service.

1 Thessalonians 5:12-13 (NIV) "[12] Now we ask you, brothers, to respect those who work hard among you, who are over you in the Lord and who admonish you. [13] Hold them in the highest regard in love because of their work. Live in peace with each other."

Hebrews 13:17 (NIV) "[17] Obey your leaders and submit to their authority. They keep watch over you as men who must give an account. Obey them so that their

work will be a joy, not a burden, for that would be of
no advantage to you."

The foundation of the "laying on of ....," and upholding it in our lives is therefor in one sense an honouring of the Lord's choosing of men and woman to lead in the affairs of the church, and an honouring of the "................................" that comes as a result of this "laying on of hands." We show that we value this foundation in our lives when we honour those whom the Lord set aside for specific purposes and upon whom hands were laid in the presence of God and the congregation.

e. The Resurrection of the dead.

The Resurrection of the dead is an essential constituent of our faith in Christ. Through embracing this truth, about the resurrection, we embrace the fact that 1. Christ rose from the dead, as He said He would, and 2. We too will rise again, either for eternal life, or unto eternal damnation.

- **Since Christ rose from the ...., we embrace the Resurrection of the dead.**

Our entire Gospel hinges on the fact that Jesus rose from the dead. He is Alive, and through Him we can truly embrace eternal life!

1 Corinthians 15:20-21 (NIV 1984) "20 But Christ has indeed been raised from the dead, the firstfruits of those who have fallen asleep. 21 For since death came through a man, the resurrection of the dead comes also through a man."

- **Since Christ died and rose from the dead our new ....is assured and affirmed.**

There is a direct connection between the resurrection of Christ and our New Birth. His Resurrection provides us with a living Hope of our New Birth.

> 1 Peter 1:3 (NIV 1984) Praise to God for a Living Hope "3 Praise be to the God and Father of our Lord Jesus Christ! In his great mercy he has given us new birth into a living hope .... the resurrection of Jesus Christ from the dead,"

- **Since Christ rose from the dead, too shall rise from the dead to .... life.**

Every Believer should live daily with this eternal hope in his or her heart, since Christ rose from the dead, we too shall rise from the dead to eternal life. We should live with this eternal hope in our hearts.

> 1 Thessalonians 4:16 (NIV 1984) "16 For the Lord himself will come down from heaven, with a loud command, with the voice of the archangel and with the trumpet call of God, and the .... in Christ will rise first."

Every Believer lives with this Eternal Hope in his or her heart, that we who are in Christ will rise again. We will also experience this resurrection Power in our lives when Christ returns.

- **By embracing the Resurrection of the dead, we embrace .... life.**

Christ came to give all who believe in Him, ... life. The essence of eternal life is that, even if we die before His second coming, we will rise again from the dead. There is life after death.

> John 3:14-16 (NKJV) "14 And as Moses lifted up the serpent in the wilderness, even so must the Son of Man be lifted up, 15 that whoever believes in

Him should not perish but have eternal life. 16
For God so loved the world that He gave His
only begotten Son, that whoever
.... in Him should not perish but
have everlasting life."

1 Corinthians 15:12-14 (NIV 1984) "12 But if it is preached
that Christ has been raised from the dead, how can
some of you say that there is no resurrection of the
dead. 13 If there is no resurrection of the dead, then
not even Christ has been raised. 14 And if Christ has
not been raised, our preaching is useless and so is
your faith."

- **By embracing the Resurrection of the dead we embrace the .... coming of Christ.**

Jesus is coming back again, and we as believers should live as those who expect to stand before Him one day and give account of our life on earth. We will be without excuse on that day since Christ paid a high price to pave the way for us to have eternal life.

Matthew 25:31-32 (NKJV) "31 "When the Son of Man
comes in His glory, and all the holy angels with Him,
then He will sit on the .... of His glory.
32 All the nations will be gathered before Him, and
He will separate them one from another, as a
shepherd divides his sheep from the goats."

Matthew 25:34 (NKJV) "34 Then the King will say to those on His right hand, 'Come, you blessed of My Father, inherit the .... prepared for you from the foundation of the world:"

Matthew 25:41(NKJV) "41 "Then He will also say to those on the left hand, 'Depart from Me, you cursed, into the everlasting .... prepared for the devil and his angels:"

Matthew 25:46 (NKJV) "46 And these will go away into everlasting ...., but the .... *into eternal life.""*

What are the key points for us to understand and appreciate?

The key points are that the way we live in this life has eternal consequences. We will all rise from the dead, whether we were Believers or not. The Believers will rise unto eternal .... and the unbelievers unto eternal .... This brings us to our next session on Eternal judgment.

1 Peter 3:10-14 (NIV) "10 But the day of the Lord will come like a thief. The heavens will disappear with a roar; the elements will be destroyed by fire, and the earth and everything in it will be laid bare. 11 Since everything will be destroyed in this way, what kind of people ought you to be? You ought to live holy and godly lives 12 as you look forward to the day of God and speed its coming. That day will bring about the destruction of the heavens by fire, and the elements will melt in the heat. 13 But in keeping with his promise we are looking forward to a new heaven and a new earth, the home of righteousness. 14 So then, dear friends, since you are looking forward to this, make every effort to be found spotless, blameless and at peace with him."

f. Eternal Judgement

The early Church counted it an essential firm foundation to establish in the daily life of every new Believer: the consciousness of eternal ....

The reward for our sins should be death on a cross. Christ made it possible that we could escape that eternal judgment by believing in Him, however, this faith should be reflected in the way in which we value His propitiation for our sins. The life we now live should be consistent with our eternal gratitude.

> John 3:16 (NIV 1984) "16 "For God so loved the world that he gave his one and only Son, that whoever believes in him shall not perish but have eternal life."

> Romans 14:10 (NIV 1984) "10 You, then, why do you judge your brother? Or why do you look down on your brother? For we will .... stand before God's judgment seat."

As people who will stand before our Lord, every Believer should embrace the following heart attitude:

1. We need to live with a .... awareness that at the end of our lives .... stand before the Throne of God, and give account of.................................., to God.

> Romans 14:12 (NIV 1984) "12 So then, ... of us will give an account of himself to God."

Sometimes people ....that we will all give an account of .... to God. Many people live as if they are beyond having to give account.

I'm sure you also live to please the One who saved you. I want to stand before Him and hear those amazing words:

"Welcome home, and well done, good, and .... servant!"

Let us live with this eternal expectation of our just reward in our hearts.

2. We need to .... our lives as those who .... have to give account for our ....

The fact remains that our words and .... are important and has a bearing on how we will spend .... One of the constant and consistent messages of the Lord Jesus to His Disciples, and then from the Apostles to the Believers in the various Churches, was the message that our faith and walk need to be consistent with the faith we profess.

Jesus one day spoke to some Scribes and Pharisees about this consistency between what people profess and the fruit they bear with their lives. He made the direct comparison with us. He said that:

"(NKJV) a tree is known by its ....," and then "How can you, being evil, speak good things? For out of the abundance of the .... the mouth speaks." These words challenged them to consider their ways, and challenges us to consider our ways. We are all on public display daily. Our lives tell a story. He went on to bring this message home by telling us that we will give account "for every idle word" we speak in "the day of judgement."

> Matthew 12:36-37 (NKJV) "36 But I say to you that for every idle word men may speak, they will give account of it in the day of judgment. 37 For by your .... you will be justified, and by your .... *you* will be condemned.""

As Believers, our words should be .... before we utter them. May the Lord help you to put aside the language of the world. I have seen, through the years, how the language of new Believers becomes one of the first signs to their unbelieving friends that things have changed. We see that the crudeness and swearing stops, the negativity is replaced with positiveness, and the lying and deceit is replaced with honestly, respect and kindness. May this be your testimony as well.

> James 2:21-24 (NIV) "[21] Was not our ancestor Abraham

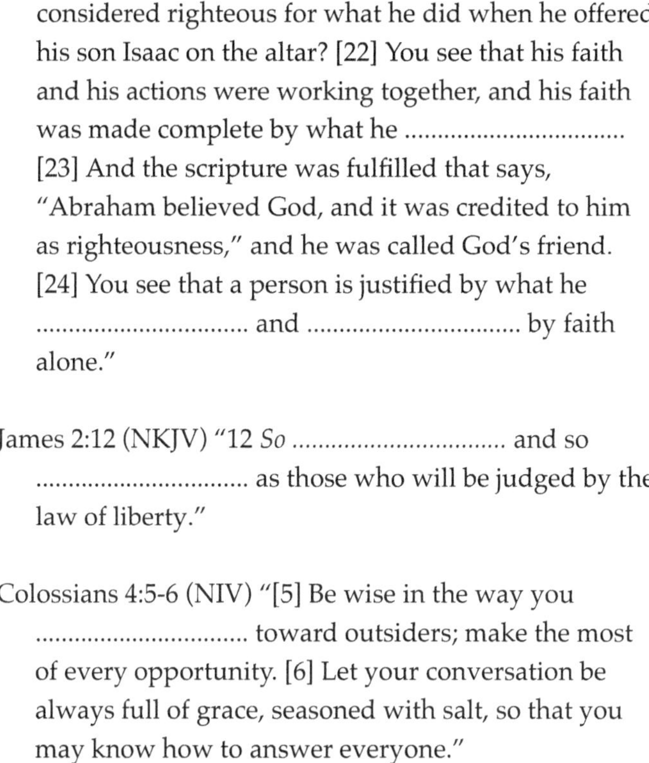

considered righteous for what he did when he offered his son Isaac on the altar? [22] You see that his faith and his actions were working together, and his faith was made complete by what he .... [23] And the scripture was fulfilled that says, "Abraham believed God, and it was credited to him as righteousness," and he was called God's friend. [24] You see that a person is justified by what he .... and .... by faith alone."

James 2:12 (NKJV) "12 *So* .... and so .... as those who will be judged by the law of liberty."

Colossians 4:5-6 (NIV) "[5] Be wise in the way you .... toward outsiders; make the most of every opportunity. [6] Let your conversation be always full of grace, seasoned with salt, so that you may know how to answer everyone."

Our lives bear witness to the life of Christ in us. May this changed life bear witness unto eternity.

3. We need to be Faithful Servants, doing what God called us to do.

One day Jesus told His Disciples a Parable on stewardship. He told them of a certain master who gave each one of his servant's talents to use. After a long while He returned and required them to give account of the talents they received. When you read this parable in Matthew 25, you quickly notice the message of how Jesus requires us to use our talents and produce a harvest. May the Lord grant that you and I use our talents to full use so that we may produce a multiplied harvest when He returns.

> Matthew 25:20-21(NKJV) "20 "So he who had received five talents came and brought five other talents, saying, 'Lord, you delivered to me five talents; look, I have gained five more talents besides them.' 21 His lord said to him, 'Well done, good and .... servant; you were .... over a few things, I will make you ruler over many things. Enter into the joy of your lord.'"

I want to stand before the Lord and hear those wonderful words: "***Well done, good and faithful servant.***"

> Ephesians 2:10 (NKJV) "10 For we are His workmanship, created in Christ Jesus for good works, which God .... beforehand that we should walk in them."

> 1 Peter 4:10-11 (NKJV) "10 As .... has received a gift, ... it to one another, as good stewards of the manifold grace of God. 11 If anyone speaks, let him speak as the oracles of God. If anyone ministers, let him do it as with the ability which God supplies, that in all things God may be glorified through Jesus Christ, to whom belong the glory and the dominion forever and ever. Amen."

Step 2 – Establish Spiritual Roots, Values and disciplines.

Once you have a "Born Again" Believer then you can start the investment process of instilling the Values of the Kingdom of God in the Believer. If you build spiritual values and disciplines into people who have never bowed their knees to the Lordship of Christ, you are building on sand. As I mentioned earlier, if you are going to build people up then make sure that you build in those lives that has Christ as their Rock and Foundation.

Values.

I always wondered where to start once people committed their lives to Christ. When I looked at how Jesus did it, remembering that He started His Discipleship journey with people who left everything to follow Him, I found that Jesus started by teaching His Disciples the Values of the Kingdom of God. One of the biggest challenges we face in ministries is sitting with people who are "churched" but never adopted and applied the values of the Kingdom of God.

Jesus' first teaching, however, was to teach His newly found Disciples the values of the Kingdom of God. Values are those virtues, which have been added into our lives by intention. Embracing and living godly values build our character. We are known by our character. We are characterised by those values we have adopted and allowed to take root in us. One famous writer suggests in one of her books that our bodies follow where our minds go. What we think about and give our attention to is what we will become. Proverbs says: "As a man think in his heart, so is he."

> Philippians 4:8 "Finally, brethren, whatsoever things are true, whatsoever things are honest, whatsoever things are just, whatsoever things are pure, whatsoever things are lovely, whatsoever things are of good report; if there be any virtue, and if there be any praise, think on these things."

The second phase of Discipleship deals with establishing roots from which our faith will grow and mature. Having strong roots are essential to growing a healthy and stable spiritual life.

Every Family has family values. Our lives are built upon these values. The Kingdom of God is established on Values. Values are roots from which one draws one's strength. This phase marks the Believer's walk as a young man or woman, as they assimilate the values of the Kingdom of God. Through the teachings of Jesus, we learnt the values He taught His Disciples.

1. Humility

Matthew 5:3 (NIV 1984) 3 "Blessed are the poor in spirit, for theirs is the kingdom of heaven."

1 Peter 5:5-6, 1 Peter 3:8, Philippians 2:3-5, Philippians 2:8.

Humility is the quality of having a modest or subjected view of one's own importance.

2. Penitence

Matthew 5:4 (NIV 1984) "4 Blessed are those who mourn, for they will be comforted."

Luke 18:13-14, Psalms 51.

Penitence is the value of reflective living. Penitence is the applied value of humbly and honestly assessing one's actions before God, with a willingness to acknowledge our wrongs and to follow through with repentance and seeking true forgiveness.

3. Meekness

Matthew 5:5 (NIV 1984) "5 Blessed are the meek, for they will inherit the earth."

James 3:13, Matthew 6:10, John 4:34, John 6:38, Isaiah 53:7.

Meekness is the consistent characteristic of submissiveness. Meekness is to present oneself in every situation as one who lives under the rule and directive of another. Meekness is to live in deference to Christ and His Word.

4. Spiritual Passion

Matthew 5:6 (NIV 1984) "6 Blessed are those who hunger and thirst for righteousness, for they will be filled."
1 Timothy 4:12, 15, Romans 12:11.

Spiritual passion is the value of giving and expressing oneself fully in one's faith.

5. Merciful

Matthew 5:7 (NIV 1984) "7 Blessed are the merciful, for they will be shown mercy."
Luke 6:36

To be Merciful is to be filled with grace towards all people, being constantly mindful of how much we've been forgiven of.

6. Purity

Matthew 5:8 (NIV 1984) "8 Blessed are the pure in heart, for they will see God."
Psalms 24:3-5, Philippians 4:8, 1 Timothy 1:5, 1 Timothy 4:12, James 4:8, 1 John 3:2-3.

Purity is characterised by freedom from immorality, adultery and sinful contamination, and is a value of the Kingdom of God.

7. Peacemakers

Matthew 5:9 (NIV 1984) "9 Blessed are the peacemakers, for they will be called sons of God."
James 3:8, Romans 14:19, Romans 12:18, Psalms 34:14, Acts 7:26, 2 Corinthians 5:19-20, Ephesians 4:3.

A peacemaker is someone who actively steps up in every adversarial situation to work towards a peaceful outcome. Peacemakers are reconciliatory in action.

There is Power in Unity. The value of living, as far as is possible from your side, at peace with people around you are actually a Characteristic of Believers.

8. Patient endurance under suffering.

> *Matthew 5:10-12 (NIV) "[10] Blessed are those who are persecuted because of righteousness, for theirs is the kingdom of heaven. "Blessed are you when people insult you, persecute you and falsely say all kinds of evil against you because of me. [12] Rejoice and be glad, because great is your reward in heaven, for in the same way they persecuted the prophets who were before you."*
>
> *Luke 6:22, 1 Peter 2:19-20, Matthew 5:38-42, Matthew 16:24, James 1:2.*

It is the ability to endure through unjust treatment because of your faith, and even go beyond the expected response to such attacks by acting in a non-retaliatory way.

Conclusion on Values

In fact, I have determined and narrowed the values down to 52 Kingdom Values. In my Book: ***"The Values of the Kingdom of God."*** I have outlined and explored these for adoption and application in our lives.

We might add the Fruit of the Spirit as values as these are often characteristics by which we are determined to be Children of God, however, these come as a direct result of the Holy Spirit's presence and pre-eminence in our lives.

> Galatians 5:22-23 (GNT) "22 But the Spirit produces love, joy, peace, patience, kindness, goodness, faithfulness,

> 23 humility, and self-control. There is no law against such things as these."

> Galatians 5:22-23 (AMPC) "22 But the fruit of the [Holy] Spirit [the work which His presence within accomplishes] is love, joy (gladness), peace, patience (an even temper, forbearance), kindness, goodness (benevolence), faithfulness, 23 Gentleness (meekness, humility), self-control (self-restraint, continence). Against such things there is no law [that can bring a charge]."

Assimilating the Values of the Kingdom of God is one thing, however, maintaining them in our lives is another, and it is therefore equally important to establish spiritual disciplines, which will ensure that these Values are kept and maintained.

Spiritual Disciplines

Spiritual disciplines are habits, practices, and experiences that are designed to develop, grow, and strengthen our inner man. Spiritual disciplines build the capacity of our character and keep the values, we aspire to assimilate into our lives, intact. Spiritual disciplines form the structure within which we train our soul to obey.

The Apostle Paul taught his disciple, Timothy, to train himself to be godly.

> 1 Timothy 4:7 (NIV) "7 Have nothing to do with godless myths and old wives' tales; rather, train yourself to be godly."

New Testament Practitioners

It seems from the impact that the early Church had that they had a few practices, which positioned them for such a revival atmosphere where people were added to the Church on a daily basis.

We also have a number of examples from that of the spiritual Disciplines of the Apostles. As the Church grew the complexities of ministry grew, however, what set the Apostles apart was their discipline to keep their Spiritual Disciplines undisturbed.

> Acts 6:4 (NIV) "4 and we will give our attention to prayer and the ministry of the word."

Acts 2 verses 42-46 highlight some of the spiritual practices of the Believers in the Book of Acts.

> Acts 2:42-47 (NIV)"42They devoted themselves to the apostles' teaching and to fellowship, to the breaking of bread and to prayer. 43 Everyone was filled with awe at the many wonders and signs performed by the apostles.44 All the believers were together and had everything in common. 45 They sold property and possessions to give to anyone who had need. 46 Every day they continued to meet together in the temple courts. They broke bread in their homes and ate together with glad and sincere hearts,47 praising God and enjoying the favor of all the people. And the Lord added to their number daily those who were being saved."

In this portion of Scripture, we observe at least ***seven spiritual disciplines***, which existed in the early Church. They practiced these disciplines daily. They gave themselves to it wholly. The Spiritual Disciplines of ***devoting yourself to the Word of God*** (Apostle's Teachings), ***worship*** (fellowship), ***Communion*** (Breaking of Bread), ***Prayer, Simplicity*** (had everything in common), ***Stewardship*** (They sold property and possessions to give to anyone who had need) and ***Witnessing*** (enjoying the favor of all the people.) The amazing thing about this testimony and example is that the Lord crowned their private and corporate devotion, by "daily adding to their numbers those who were being saved."

Kingdom of God Spiritual disciplines.

Along with teaching His Disciples the Values of the Kingdom of God, Jesus taught His Disciples Spiritual Disciplines. He knew that these values would only remain if maintained and undergirded by well-established spiritual disciplines.

1. Prayer: Jesus offered us, and His Disciples advice on the spiritual discipline of prayer. He often taught them on this spiritual discipline and He Himself modelled it to them.

> Matthew 6:6-8 (NIV) "6 But when you pray, go into your room, close the door and pray to your Father, who is unseen. Then your Father, who sees what is done in secret, will reward you. 7 And when you pray, do not keep on babbling like pagans, for they think they will be heard because of their many words. 8 Do not be like them, for your Father knows what you need before you ask him."

2. Fasting: Jesus also taught us on the Spiritual Discipline of Fasting in Matthew 6 verses 16-17. Jesus fasted 40 days prior to His earthly ministry started. We've upheld this practice of Fasting at the beginning of every year, for many years now.

> Matthew 6:16-17 (NIV) 16 "When you fast, do not look sombre as the hypocrites do, for they disfigure their faces to show others they are fasting. Truly I tell you, they have received their reward in full. 17 But when you fast, put oil on your head and wash your face,

3. Stewardship: Jesus taught us on the Spiritual Discipline of Stewardship in Matthew 6 verses 2-4, and through the Parable of the Talents in Matthew 25 verses 14 -30.

On one occasion He taught them that good stewardship is to pay their taxes in Matthew 22 verses 15 to 22. These are of course just a snippet of an in depth study on Stewardship.

> Matthew 6:2-4 (NIV) 2 "So when you give to the needy, do not announce it with trumpets, as the hypocrites do in the synagogues and on the streets, to be honored by others. Truly I tell you, they have received their reward in full. 3 But when you give to the needy, do not let your left hand know what your right hand is doing, 4 so that your giving may be in secret. Then your Father, who sees what is done in secret, will reward you.

> Matthew 25:14, 20-21 (NKJV) The Parable of the Talents "14 "For the kingdom of heaven is like a man traveling to a far country, who called his own servants and delivered his goods to them." 20 "So he who had received five talents came and brought five other talents, saying, 'Lord, you delivered to me five talents; look, I have gained five more talents besides them.' 21 His lord said to him, 'Well done, good and faithful servant; you were faithful over a few things, I will make you ruler over many things. Enter into the joy of your lord.'"

> Matthew 22:21 (NKJV) "21 They said to Him, "Caesar's." And He said to them, "Render therefore to Caesar the things that are Caesar's, and to God the things that are God's."

4. Reading, Meditating and Practicing the Word of God: Jesus taught us the Spiritual Discipline of having an intake of the Word of God on a Daily Basis.

During His days of Testing, Jesus used the Word to defend and persevere through the temptations Satan tried on Him. Jesus quoted Deuteronomy 8 verse 3 that: "Man shall not live by bread alone, but by every Word that proceeds from the mouth of God." Jesus presented Himself as the Bread of Life. Every New Testament Book endorses and encourages us to embrace the Words of the Lord on a daily basis.

> Luke 4:4 (NKJV) "4 But Jesus answered him, saying, "It is written, 'Man shall not live by bread alone, but by every word of God.'"

> Psalms 1:1-3 NIV "1 Blessed is the one who does not walk in step with the wicked or stand in the way that sinners take or sit in the company of mockers,2 but whose delight is in the law of the Lord, and who meditates on his law day and night. 3 That person is like a tree planted by streams of water, which yields its fruit in season and whose leaf does not wither—whatever they do prospers."

5. Worship: Jesus taught His Disciples the discipline of worship.

The first part of the "***Lord's Prayer***" is devoted to "***Hallowing Our Father in Heaven***." In the Gospel of John He teaches us that the Father is "***looking for worshippers.***" On one occasion He even said that if the disciples would cease to shout out His praises that "these stones would cry out."

God dwells in the praises of His people. The First commandment is to "***love the Lord your God with all your heart, with all your soul, with all your mind, and with all your strength.***" What better way is there to take time to worship Him on a daily basis and to give expression of your love for the Lord.

John 4:23-24 (NKJV) 23 But the hour is coming, and now is, when the true worshipers will worship the Father in spirit and truth; for the Father is seeking such to worship Him. 24 God is Spirit, and those who worship Him must worship in spirit and truth.

Mark 12:29-30 (NKJV) 29 Jesus answered him, "The first of all the commandments is: 'Hear, O Israel, the Lord our God, the Lord is one. 30 And you shall love the Lord your God with all your heart, with all your soul, with all your mind, and with all your strength. 'This is the first commandment.

6. Simplicity: Jesus taught His Disciples on the Spiritual Discipline of Simplicity.

He encouraged His Disciples to live simple lives without pursuing earthly treasures. The early Church lived such simple lives. We see that they sold their lands and houses and had everything in common. They laid their treasures at the feet of the Apostles, thus laying up treasures in Heaven. Their treasures were laid up in Kingdom Advancing pursuits. When He sent out His Disciples, He sent them out with a few simple instructions in Matthew 10. They were not to take with them a purse or extra sets of clothing. This is truly living a simple life.

Matthew 10:9-10 (NKJV) 9 Provide neither gold nor silver nor copper in your money belts, 10 nor bag for your journey, nor two tunics, nor sandals, nor staffs; for a worker is worthy of his food.

When Jesus taught His Disciples on the mountain, He encouraged them to rather lay-up treasures for themselves in heaven, thus discouraging them to live lives full of treasures here.

Matthew 6:19-21 (NKJV) 19 "Do not lay up for yourselves treasures on earth, where moth and rust destroy and

> where thieves break in and steal; 20 but lay up for yourselves treasures in heaven, where neither moth nor rust destroys and where thieves do not break in and steal. 21 For where your treasure is, there your heart will be also."

The Apostle Paul speaks about contentment.

> 1 Timothy 6:6-8 (NKJV) "6 Now godliness with contentment is great gain. 7 For we brought nothing into this world, and it is certain we can carry nothing out. 8 And having food and clothing, with these we shall be content."

7. Servanthood: Jesus taught His Disciples the Spiritual Discipline of Servanthood.

If you have Kingdom advancing aspirations, it is best done along the pathway of service to your fellow man.

> Mark 9:35 (NKJV) "35 And He sat down, called the twelve, and said to them, "If anyone desires to be first, he shall be last of all and servant of all."

Jesus modelled this in a number of ways. He served humanity by His death and resurrection. He served His Disciples by giving them the Words of Life. He laid His life down for His sheep. Serving is giving yourself wholly for a cause. It is the applying of all your mental, physical and emotional faculties for the cause of advancing the Kingdom of God through our active engagement with people in and out of the Kingdom of God.

8. Obedience: Jesus taught His Disciples the Spiritual Discipline of Obedience.

Part of the process of Discipleship is to teach our disciples "***to obey everything***" Jesus taught us.

> Matthew 28:20 (NKJV) "20 teaching them to observe all things that I have commanded you; and lo, I am with you always, even to the end of the age." Amen."

Jesus practiced and modelled obedience unto death. Our disciplines are not just for a season or for a specific event, but it is an inward aptitude of discipline for this life.

Jesus learnt obedience through His suffering. Disciplining ourselves daily towards submission and obedience to the Word, Will and Purpose of God will most certainly unlock great favour and blessing over our lives. This is the Promise God gave us in Deuteronomy 28 verses 1-13.

Conclusion on Spiritual Disciplines.

There are many spiritual disciplines to explore and assimilate into our daily lives. The Spiritual Disciplines of Fasting and Prayer, Stewardship, Simplicity, Servanthood, studying and meditating on the Word of God, are some of the most valued disciplines to uphold. You can read more on these in my Book on "The Values and Spiritual Disciplines of the Kingdom of God." Spiritual disciplines will keep the fire of God burning ablaze inside of you.

3. Step 3 – Discovering and developing our Spiritual Gifts and developing ministry skills to fulfil God's Purpose on our lives.

The third phase of Discipleship deals with us discovering and developing our spiritual gifts, where we develop ministry skills to fulfil our calling in service of the Lord and we continue to grow strong and healthy roots to ensure that we, both bring forth healthy fruit, as well as withstand the evil temptation of the enemy.

Character Building happens when we apply the Values of the Word of God on a consistent basis. This is the phase where we become overcomers by the Confession of our mouths and the application of the Word of God. This stage is also marked by our skill and gift development. This is a continuation of the "Young men" phase.

1. Spiritual Gift Discovery Course. Weekend Encounter.
2. Survey of the Bible Course. Weekend Encounter.
3. How to share your Faith Course. Weekend Encounter.
4. Overcoming Course. Weekend Encounter.
5. Shepherd, Group Leader Training Course. Weekend Encounter.

These five weekend encounters are designed to help the Disciples develop skills and abilities that would assist them in fulfilling the purpose of God in their lives.

1. Spiritual Gift Discovery Course.

God has gifted each one of us with spiritual gifts for the purpose of building each other up in our faith. This course is designed to help the Disciple discover the Gifts of God upon their lives. These are distinctly different from natural gifts, although there is often some confluence between them. Once they discover their spiritual gifts, they are taught how to develop and avail themselves to be used by God in them to the building up of the Church.

> 1 Corinthians 7:7 (NIV) "7 I wish that all of you were as I am. But each of you has your own gift from God; one has this gift, another has that."

> 1 Peter 4:10 (NIV) "10 Each of you should use whatever gift you have received to serve others, as faithful stewards of God's grace in its various forms."

2. Survey of the Bible Course.

Weekend. Since most of our Disciples are new to the faith, we need to help them understand the message of the Bible in its entirety. The best way is to give them a crash course over a weekend and take them through the Bruce Wilkerson course, "Walk through the Bible." I highly recommend this course, at this phase in the discipling process.

3. How to share your Faith Course.

We are all witnesses of what God did in our lives. Our call is to testify of what He has done in our lives and continue to do.

4. Overcoming Course.

This course is designed to uproot lingering roots from our past such as Fear, Unforgiveness, Rejection and Resentment. If there still remains any areas in our Disciples' lives where worldliness remains, these are dealt with during this weekend. The Bible outlines the extent of these in Matthew 13 in the Parable of the Sower. Interestingly, the thorns only become a threat to the growth of the seed when it is due to reproduce. It is therefor fitting that once you've developed spiritual values and disciplines, that you uproot those "cares of the world," and "thorns" that might choke the Word inside of the Believers and keep them from becoming fruitful.

> Matthew 13:22 (NKJV) "22 Now he who received seed among the thorns is he who hears the word, and the cares of this world and the deceitfulness of riches choke the word, and he becomes unfruitful."

5. Shepherd, Group Leader Course.

Once you've led two or more people to Christ, you need to gather them, like Jesus did with His Disciples, to teach them. This might be a wonderful experience for your disciples as they meet with you, the experienced one, weekly, but daunting as they contemplate reproducing that with their own. This course will help them understand that it is really the Holy Spirit who bring this transformation and life changes in people's lives, and that you and I are simply facilitators in the work of God.

> Acts 20:28 (NIV) "28 Keep watch over yourselves and all the flock of which the Holy Spirit has made you overseers. Be shepherds of the church of God, which he bought with his own blood."

As this Scripture highlights, being a Shepherd, or group Leader, is an honourable appointment by the Holy Spirit. This is both a huge responsibility and honour to be entrusted with the welfare of God's own Children's lives. This course helps our Disciples learn the skills to do so with excellence.

4. Step 4 – Discipling Fruit-producers.

The fourth phase of Discipleship deals with us bearing Fruit, through consistently putting into practice what we've learnt, and by living a life of love worth following, and shepherding those entrusted to our care.

This Step is all about producing fruit through application of learnt experiences and Gift discovery and use. I am always excited about this phase since it is always great to disciple obedient practitioners. At this stage of the journey, they are mature and diligent followers of the Lord Jesus. They are accountable.

1. Walking with purpose.

Build purposeful relationships. Finding Worthy Men/Woman (Matthew 10:11, 2 Timothy 2:2.)

It is important to constantly keep your Disciples focused, and one of those key areas is to keep them focused on souls, and more specifically on finding "worthy men and woman" to advance the Kingdom of God.

2. Priesthood. Praying effffectively.

During this phase we take our Disciples one step deeper in their walk with God by teaching them to be Priests. This far they learned and practiced personal prayer, but that is not all that God planned for them in regard to prayer. God desires them to be a "Holy Priesthood." One of the key functions of a Priest is to make intercession on behalf of those entrusted to our care.

3. Caring compassionately.

It is such an honour to be entrusted with one of the precious sheep in God's fold. Our gratitude is shown in the way in which we care for those entrusted to us. Learn to be a "Good Shepherd." Every man of God carries this care in their hearts for God's people.

4. Walking worthily.

As we grow in our Faith, and our responsibility and accountability increase, so does our consciousness to walk worthily according to the trust God placed in us. As you increase in fruitfulness and more souls look to you for guidance, directions and an example to follow, you need to think and rethink how you speak, what you say and do, and what example you want others to follow. We constantly consider our ways, actions, whereabouts, especially as to how they might advance the Kingdom of God. We are Christ's Ambassadors!

5. Walking in the Spirit.

During this phase of Discipleship, we teach our Disciples the value of a consistent walk under the direction and guidance of the Holy Spirit since He is our Helper and the most powerful partner in our ministry. Without His work in our lives, no sanctification can take place.

Without His work in our ministry, we will see no fruit on our labours. He changes hearts. He Heals, delivers and convicts. Walking in fellowship with the Holy Spirit has many providential advantages since He is our ultimate Teacher. It is His Anointing on our lives that makes all the difference.

6. Practicing hospitality.

One of the requirements for an Elder is that he or she needs to be hospitable. Having a clean house that is always open to those who need to come over for a chat, prayer or some ministry is essentials. Keeping your house clean and presentable is always a good indication of one's diligence in discipline. You don't need to necessarily cook every time people come over, but a simple glass of water when they arrive goes a long way in presenting yourself as a good host. Cleanliness and hospitality are two key essentials as an aspiring Christian Leader.

5. Step 5 – Multiplying the Body.

The fifth step of Discipleship deals with our Disciples multiplying themselves through their Disciples, by helping and guiding them to consistently put into practice what they've learnt through their union with Christ. We model it to them, and they model it to their Disciples, by living a life of love worth following, and shepherding them into their purpose.

1. Fruitfulness and Multiplication.

The fifth step in the process of developing as a disciple is to develop in the gifts and graces upon our lives until we become fruitful and through us the Kingdom of God starts multiplying, disciples.

Fruitfulness refers to the ability of a disciple to win souls for Christ. Multiplication refers to the disciples to make fruit-producing disciples.

Genesis 1:28 (KJV) "[28] And God blessed them, and God

said unto them, Be fruitful, and multiply, and replenish the earth, and subdue it: and have dominion over the fish of the sea, and over the fowl of the air, and over every living thing that moveth upon the earth."

Genesis 17:6 (KJV) "[6] And I will make the exceeding fruitful, and I will make nations of thee, and kings shall come out of thee."

Genesis 28:3-4 (KJV) "[3] And God Almighty bless thee, and make thee fruitful, and multiply thee, that thou mayest be a multitude of people; [4] And give thee the blessing of Abraham, to thee, and to thy seed with thee; that thou mayest inherit the land wherein thou art a stranger, which God gave unto Abraham."

Matthew 3:8 (NIV) "[8] Produce fruit in keeping with repentance."

2. Reproducing through others.

The key elements of this step in the process of Discipleship are to reproduce and multiply the Body of Christ through strengthening and encouraging your Disciples to be models and worthy examples to their Disciples, as well as help your disciples to being fruitful and to multiply. Through this step we equip our Disciples to go higher and deeper in their own walk with God.

This course was designed to assist fruit-producing disciples to live a life that will encourage a lifetime of fruitfulness. It will also give our disciples skills and guidelines to navigate their disciples through seasons of challenge and growth. This course is packed with Leadership advancing principles. The more these areas are addressed and encouraged, the more we will experience growth and multiplication. We explore:

1. Vision and dreams.

2. Set Godly Goals.
3. Character development
4. Gifts development - Impartation and Activation
5. Fruitfulness comes through constant challenge.
6. Relationships - Family, Children and Friends
7. The Power of encouragement
8. Finances - Personal and Ministry finances
9. Dealing with setbacks

- How to deal with failure?
- How to deal with betrayal?
- How to deal with rejection?
- How to deal with trials?
- How to deal with despondency?

10. Eternal rewards

In Conclusion on the Disciple making process, this is not conclusive, as we constantly have new emphasis highlighted to us by the Holy Spirit.

8

PHASE THREE - CONGREGATING THE DISCIPLESHIP GROUPS

Phase Three marks the formalisation of the next step in planting a dynamic Church and that is congregating the Discipleship Groups. Once your Disciples are proving to be putting into practice what you've been teaching them then they will be fruitful. Once they lead people to Christ, they gather them into groups to disciple them effectively.

Once you have at least three discipleship groups going other than the one you're leading then you can proceed with Phase Three activities.

1. Formulating the Church constitution for the Church structure, and office bearers

Having a soundly formulated Church Constitution will harness you against many harmful false doctrines, which go around. You will be wise to think through and receive wise council before you formalise your church Constitution.

2. Organizing the Leaders. Appointing Elders

By this time of the Church Planting journey, you would be intimately aware of the strengths and weaknesses of your Leaders. You will also be aware of God's greater purpose on your Disciple's lives and of course you would by now have seen their abilities and capacities to reproduce and how they run under pressure.

In consistence with your pursuit to develop the right DNA in your Church, appoint only Leaders who are fruitful and carry the right heart for the harvest and to making disciples. I choose some of them, after prayer, to be the first elders of the Church.

3. Organizing Administration and Key staff

Depending on the size of your Church Planting vision, you might need some key staff to prepare for your public launch. Most Apostolic Leaders need administrative assistance. It is therefore vital that you look for someone who would serve in a volunteer capacity as a Church Secretary. They could assist you with appointment coordination, database formulation and upkeep, simple letters processing, and documentary profiling and processing.

The first staff, volunteer or paid, should be at minimum: a Personal Assistant, a Worship Leader and worship team of at least three people including the Leader, a Tech person to handle the Sound, lights, projection, recording and technical setup and coordination. The tech person will need at least two assistants to help with setup, even if you're in a permanent facility. You will need a Children and/or Youth Leader with at least as many assistants as what you have Discipleship groups. This person can serve both leadership roles for a start, however, as the ministry grows you might consider employing a full-time worker to oversee at least one Key Leader over each of these two areas. Consistent with our vision to continue with a strong emphasis on corporate outreach you might consider employing an Evangelistic Outreach leader to coordinate the Church's outreach programs. Outreach is the ministry of every person, however, to make a maximum impact in your area we coordinate our efforts. These would most certainly fulfill your initial demands for establishing a sound, well-rounded team.

4. Formulizing the liturgy for the congregational services

Determining both the order and progression within the services, as well as determining the worship style is of utmost importance prior to launching the church publicly. Thinking through the long-term vision, it is far more expedient to set a liturgical order that would serve the church well for future multiplication into multiple services, than having them run for as long as what it takes. Rather limit these services to around 90 minutes, than having them too long and too hard to multiply.

Also, determine the kind of worship style and songs you will have in your celebration services prior to starting. If you don't set the platform, it might become an unhealthy distraction down the road.

The key elements for meeting together "in His Name" are Worship, Prayer, The Reading and Ministry of the Word, Communion, pastoral / salvation / care ministry, and notifications.

5. Developing a plan for Acts 1 verse 8 witnessing

God called us to be His witnesses in Jerusalem, Judea, Samaria, and the ends of the earth. Be determined to lead your church to touch and engage all four of these areas right from the onset of your ministry launch. Jerusalem is the sub-culture that you primarily minister to. This is the primary and prominent group your launch discipleship group consist of. The Judean group is that people group who are the same is your primary group, but reside far away in another city or town, but in the same country, province or state. Samaria refers to the people group that is different from your primary group yet live in close vicinity to where the core group live. These might be other cultural or ethnic group. The ends of the earth are exactly that, mission outreaches to people who are both different and distant from your group. God anointed and called us to be His witnesses to all. Be intentional about having a plan, and most importantly, that you lead it at this point of your church planting journey.

6. Organising disciples into body ministry areas

By this time of your Church Planting process all your Disciples would have completed Phase Three of Discipleship Journeys. They would be familiar with and developing their Gifts and Skills. Encourage them to operate under the guidance of the Holy Spirit to build up their Disciples, and as they have seen, experienced and received Holy Spirit ministry from you, let them minister under that same anointing. Create opportunities where they are able to minister to the larger, combined groups as well, but in an orderly and edifying way.

7. Finding the right place to bring everyone together

Up to this point the ministry primarily took place in your, and your disciple's homes. It is time to look for a suitable place to congregate all the discipleship groups on a regular basis. God desires His people to meet together regularly. Unless you have the resources to buy land and build, or to buy a suitable facility, you might have to start in a temporary meeting place. I have started churches like this in rented places many times in my life. I know some churches that grew to tens of thousands before they ever ventured into buying land.

What is important to look for?

Since this will become the secondary "window" into the "church," is your location, and the way you present yourself to the world. One of the many advantages of planting a church in this way is that after six to nine months you should have some funds saved up to do the things that need to be done for taking the church public.

The right location would be a place that is normally used for gathering people like a School Hall, Hotel Conference facility or Community Hall, provided that they present well and have a "safe" feel to them. Avoid using clubs or facilities that are close or associated with Bars, Clubs or Sports facilities. These don't carry the right atmosphere and are often used for functions that might leave you running around on Sunday mornings to get the place cleaned out and prepared as a place of worship. Ask God to direct you to the right place and choose wisely.

8. Organizing Diaconia.

Organize the rest of your disciples, and their disciples to serve as deacons during the first phase of the church's public launch. You need people to assist with set up and preparation for your joint services. You need a Set up and Pack up team, a Welcoming team, an Ushering team to receive, count and bank the tithes and offerings, and if you're in an urban area you might need Carpark attendants to direct traffic and people before and after services. The rule of thumb is to have one Carpark attendant for every 12 discipleship groups. You will need a Hospitality team to serve refreshments like water, coffee and tea. You will need a Follow-up Team to get in contact with visitors and connect them with their closest Elder to direct them to the best new Discipleship group. You need a Clean-up Team to leave the facilities in a better condition as what you've found it each week.

9. Formulizing Systems.

Our bodies function with coordinated systems like a digestive system, cardio-vascular system, respiratory system, and neurological system. Each one of these functions independently from each other yet if any one of them fail, our whole body fail. It is the same in planting a dynamic church; you need all the systems in place for it to function in a healthy and progressive way.

The systems that are essential to planting a dynamic church are Administrative System, Financial System, Care System, Outreach System, Worship System, Prayer and Devotions System, Missions System, and Welfare System.

Phase Four – Church launching Phase.

This phase is landmarked by the Discipleship Groups congregating for Weekly Worship, observing the Sacraments and Celebration. During this phase we start seeing this body of Believers going public as a unified Body where each one does its part to build the Church up. During this phase the Church mobilizes herself into a corporate harvesting machine. By maintaining the DNA of Discipleship and keeping its focus on seeking and saving the lost, the church will traject herself on a pathway of continued growth. You will find Timothy's raised, Paul's released, and the Kingdom of God expanding in various and wonderful ways.

Phase Five – Multiplication.

1. Mobilizing Timothy's.

Some of those whom God will give you as Disciples will be Timothy's. They will be spiritual sons to you and even though you will send them out to plant new churches, they will always remain with you. These spiritual sons are huge blessings in one's life. As a Father of five daughters, I have a dream of seeing my children succeed and accomplish bigger and better things than I did. As a Spiritual Father, I have the same vision and dream for my Spiritual Sons and daughters. Mobilize to see that vision become a reality.

2. Releasing Paul's.

Some of the Disciples God raised up under your ministry will leave you to go on to lead their own ministries. Thank God in advance for the privilege that you had to play a role in their growth and development. Releasing the "Paul's" could be a very painful experience.

Rather prepare yourself in advance that some of the people you pour your life into might leave you at an unexpected point to start their own ministries. Rather expect it than be surprised by it. Release the Paul's!

3. Multiplication strategies.

The best multiplication strategies are those that are prayerfully planned and prepared.

9

UNDERSTANDING THE CHALLENGES IN CHURCH PLANTING

Church planting is exciting, but costly. To see visions fulfilled will cost you. There is a price to pay to see successful churches planted. Committing to be a Church Planter, or engaging in the ministry of Planting Churches, is committing to a life of great sacrifices, however, the cost of being a Church Planter is outweighed by the eternal treasures stored up for us who faithfully follow the dream of God for our lives.

Jesus, in His first teaching of His Disciples laid this Foundation. He equipped them; to be prepared to for all kinds of persecutions, abuse, slander, evil speaking, mistreatment and even death. He prepared them, with a reminder that "the prophets were persecuted in the same way."

> Matthew 5:10-12 (NIV) "10 Blessed are those who are persecuted because of righteousness, for theirs is the kingdom of heaven. 11 "Blessed are you when people insult you, persecute you and falsely say all kinds of evil against you because of me. 12 Rejoice and be glad, because great is your reward in heaven, for in

> the same way they persecuted the prophets who were before you."

In this session, I will focus my attention to the challenges and sacrifices to be considered by every Church Planter. I just want you to be better prepared for the journey you're about to undertake. Beyond the excitement of being involved in something great, there is the sobering reality of the dual natural and spiritual oppositions we will face in seeing these wonderful visions fulfilled.

Successful Church planting requires monetary resources, people resources, skill resources and equipment resources, and sometimes some of these are simply lacking. These are some of the things that might cost you money, but then there are the time, relationship and energy commitment costs, which are not always clearly outlined and defined. Beyond the monetary challenges lies a spiritual and emotional battle. I pray that you will find yourself equipped and better prepared for some of the challenges you might face in days and years to come.

1. Loneliness and isolation.

One of the challenges, which many, if not most of us, will face, is that of loneliness and isolation. Since the call of God often takes most of us out of our "Father's land" to a place where God wants to use us for His Glory, it unfortunately also brings alongside this separation, the feeling of loneliness and isolation.

For Abraham it was leaving his country, his family and his Father's house. The cost for Abraham to see the promise of God fulfilled meant that he had to leave his heritage, his country and family.

> Genesis 12:1-4 (NIV) 1 The Lord had said to Abram, "Go
> from your country, your people and your father's
> household to the land I will show you. 2 "I will make
> you into a great nation, and I will bless you; I will
> make your name great, and you will be a blessing. 3 I
> will bless those who bless you, and whoever curses

you I will curse; and all peoples on earth will be blessed through you." 4 So Abram went, as the Lord had told him; and Lot went with him. Abram was seventy-five years old when he set out from Harran."

Church Planting and following the Call of God can be a difficult experience and, in many ways, leave you, and the members of your family, feeling lonely and isolated. For us, it is sometimes easier since we have a sense of purpose in obeying the Call of God, but for our loved ones, it is sometimes a different experience. Take time to take care of their needs as they come to terms with their new country or environment.

2. Desertions and Betrayal.

One of the toughest challenges in Church Planting is when key staff or people you love, trusted and invested in, suddenly leave the fellowship. This could be for known or unknown reasons. People leave for all kinds of reasons. It still hurts when they decide to leave, and often we find that it causes an unsettling within the fellowship, especially if they occupied key leadership positions.

The Apostle Paul had such an encounter once, just as they set out on a Holy Spirit inspired mission in Acts 13. Soon after their first mission, as they left Paphos and arrived in Perga, one of the team members left the team. This was such a setback for Paul that later when Barnabas wanted to bring John Mark back, he refused.

Acts 13:13 (NIV) "13 From Paphos, Paul and his companions sailed to Perga in Pamphylia, where John left them to return to Jerusalem."

Acts 15:37-40 (NIV) "37 Barnabas wanted to take John, also called Mark, with them, 38 but Paul did not think it wise to take him, because he had deserted them in Pamphylia and had not continued with them in the

> work. 39 They had such a sharp disagreement that they parted company. Barnabas took Mark and sailed for Cyprus, 40 but Paul chose Silas and left, commended by the believers to the grace of the Lord."

Paul did not want John Mark back on the team since he deserted them back in Pamphylia. Sometimes it hurts so much when someone deserts the team that it is hard to let him or her come back and act as if things are fine. This is something you and I need to prepare ourselves for. We too might have people deserting our mission. I can tell you, it's hard, I've had dear friends simply desert us while we stepped out in faith to pursue what God called us to do. The worst part is that it is done without explanation. I pray that you too will find comfort from the Lord, as you pour your pain and heartache out before Him.

Of course, the most painful of separations happen when people not only desert you but do so intentionally to hurt you and then betray the trust you've given them and cause even greater hurt and division, and this often leads into painful church and relationship splits. I always encourage myself through the experience Jesus had with Judas Iscariot. Live honourably, speak wisely, keep yourself from speaking about others in a derogatory or demeaning way, never gossip, but speak only about others what will be uplifting, encouraging and endorsing. In this way keep your life less susceptible to unkind betrayals of trust. It might not absolve you from going through it, but at least the impact will be less severe.

3. Plots and divisions.

When Paul and Barnabas went to Iconium they had tremendous success, however, some of the Jews did not believe the Message they preached, and they started poisoning the minds of the people and plotted to have Paul and Barnabas stoned.

It never ceases to amaze me that in the midst of God doing incredible miracles through the lives of His servants, that the enemy would come in through so-called "Believers" and stir up strive, form plots and intentionally cause divisions to harm the works of God.

> Acts 14:1-5 (NIV) "At Iconium Paul and Barnabas went as usual into the Jewish synagogue. There they spoke so effectively that a great number of Jews and Greeks believed. 2 But the Jews who refused to believe stirred up the other Gentiles and poisoned their minds against the brothers. 3 So Paul and Barnabas spent considerable time there, speaking boldly for the Lord, who confirmed the message of his grace by enabling them to perform signs and wonders. 4 The people of the city were divided; some sided with the Jews, others with the apostles. 5 There was a plot afoot among both Gentiles and Jews, together with their leaders, to mistreat them and stone them."

The key is to release those who hurt you by forgiving them like Jesus forgave those who harmed Him. When they stoned Stephen, his last words echo in my heart: "Please forgive them for they don't know what they are doing." The sooner you bring yourself to a place of releasing those who hurt you, the quicker you can move on. Do not get entrenched by the evil deeds and actions of others, rather, let our resolve be that God will bring vindication for us.

4. Persecution.

On another occasion it was the Jewish Leaders who incited the woman of high standing in Pisidian Antioch to persecute Paul and Barnabas.

> Acts 13:49-50 (NIV) 9 The word of the Lord spread through the whole region. 50 But the Jewish leaders incited the God-fearing women of high standing and the leading men of the city. They stirred up persecution against Paul and Barnabas, and expelled them from their region.

Jesus warned us about being persecuted for doing good and doing His will in Matthew chapter 5. He called us blessed who endure such evil treatment.

> Matthew 5:10-12 (NIV) "10 Blessed are those who are persecuted because of righteousness, for theirs is the kingdom of heaven. 11 "Blessed are you when people insult you, persecute you and falsely say all kinds of evil against you because of me. 12 Rejoice and be glad, because great is your reward in heaven, for in the same way they persecuted the prophets who were before you."

I recently listened to a dear friend of mine telling me of the persecution he and his family have endured in Vietnam for preaching the Good News of Jesus Christ. Even though they have endured so much physical and emotional persecution, their spirits are up, and they continue steadfastly in preaching the Gospel. They have endured physical beatings, long periods of strenuous imprisonments where they were malnourished, left for dead, yet God is faithful, and He continues to help them. May our spirits be strong to endure such persecutions as well.

5. Imprisonment.

One of the hardest things is to find yourself behind bars, in prison, for your stand for the cause of Christ. The Apostles Paul and Peter were no strangers to finding themselves flogged and imprisoned. On no occasion do we read that they bemoaned their situation, rather the opposite. We frequently read of them worshipping the Lord and witnessing even when they have good reason to be downcast. The Apostle Paul even counted it a privilege. On a few occasions we read of how God sent His Angels to deliver His Apostles from prison. We have record of at least two occasions where God delivered Peter from prison. Once in Acts chapter five, and once in chapter twelve, and then we read about Paul and Silas' experience in prison.

Acts 5:18-20 (NIV) 18 They arrested the apostles and put them in the public jail. 19 But during the night an angel of the Lord opened the doors of the jail and brought them out. 20 "Go, stand in the temple courts," he said, "and tell the people all about this new life."

Acts 12:5-9 (NIV) "5 So Peter was kept in prison, but the church was earnestly praying to God for him. 6 The night before Herod was to bring him to trial, Peter was sleeping between two soldiers, bound with two chains, and sentries stood guard at the entrance. 7 Suddenly an angel of the Lord appeared and a light shone in the cell. He struck Peter on the side and woke him up. "Quick, get up!" he said, and the chains fell off Peter's wrists. 8 Then the angel said to him, "Put on your clothes and sandals. "And Peter did so. "Wrap your cloak around you and follow me," the angel told him. 9 Peter followed him out of the prison, but he had no idea that what the angel was doing was really happening; he thought he was seeing a vision."

Acts 16:23-26 (NIV) 23 After they had been severely flogged, they were thrown into prison, and the jailer was commanded to guard them carefully. 24 When he received these orders, he put them in the inner cell and fastened their feet in the stocks. 25 About midnight Paul and Silas were praying and singing hymns to God, and the other prisoners were listening to them. 26 Suddenly there was such a violent earthquake that the foundations of the prison were shaken. At once all the prison doors flew open, and everyone's chains came loose.

Things have not changed much since Joseph was put into prison for the Integrity he upheld. During the ages Prophets and Apostles alike endured this kind of hostile treatment from opposing forces. There are thousands of Christian Leaders behind prison bars today for the faith they upheld. May we who share some kind of a freedom where we share our faith never forget that others pay a high price for the faith they profess.

6. Killing and flogging.

John the Baptist, a Great Man of God, lost his live in a show-off charade by a king. The senseless murdering of Men of God is quite outrageous. Many have lost their lives as a result of their stand in faith. Abel was one of the first ones to lose his life over an offering that was acceptable to God. They tried to kill Joseph. In the New Testament we read about the beheading of John the Baptist. King Herod had James, the Brother of James Killed. Stephen, a man full of the Holy Spirit, was stoned to death.

> Acts 7:59-60 (NIV) "59 While they were stoning him,
> Stephen prayed, "Lord Jesus, receive my spirit." 60
> Then he fell on his knees and cried out, "Lord, do not
> hold this sin against them. "When he had said this, he
> fell asleep."

> Acts 12:1-2 (NIV) "1 It was about this time that King
> Herod arrested some who belonged to the church,
> intending to persecute them. 2 He had James, the
> brother of John, put to death with the sword."

These kinds of brutalities are recorded in Hebrews:

> Hebrews 11:35-40 (NIV) 35 Women received back their
> dead, raised to life again. There were others who were
> tortured, refusing to be released so that they might
> gain an even better resurrection. 36 Some faced jeers
> and flogging, and even chains and imprisonment. 37

> They were put to death by stoning; they were sawed
> in two; they were killed by the sword. They went
> about in sheepskins and goatskins, destitute,
> persecuted and mistreated— 38 the world was not
> worthy of them. They wandered in deserts and
> mountains, living in caves and in holes in the ground.
> 39 These were all commended for their faith, yet none
> of them received what had been promised, 40 since
> God had planned something better for us so that only
> together with us would they be made perfect.

It seems, from this account, that life will be hard, and persecution guaranteed if you're an ardent follower of Jesus. May our journey along the pathways of history bring both an appreciation for when we are able to share our faith without the potential of such escalated persecutions, as well as a preparedness that, if we had to face such tribulations, that we will be ready to embrace it, not as if something unique and strange has come on us, but rather that we too have been found worthy of following the Lord in this kind of severe persecutions.

7. Hardships.

We frequently read how the Apostle Paul exhorts the Believers, and his Disciples, to endure hardship. Hardship can come in many forms. Hardship could be the adversity one faces, for doing what God called you to do, or by those who oppose the Message you bring. Some hardships come through people and some through the fall-out with people or institutional problems. It might lead us into poverty, destitution, suffering, difficulty and discomfort. Hardships are those hard to comprehend; "I don't know what is happening" times in our ministries. Hardships are those troublesome times when all we need to do is keep on walking even if we don't understand.

Paul exhorts Timothy to keep his head in all circumstances and to endure the hardships he will face. One of the things about hardships is that they make you question yourself, your teachings, your actions and words. It is so important to keep a sound mind during those times of serious reflections, hence Paul's advice to "keep your head in all situations."

> 2 Timothy 4:5 (NIV) 5 But you, keep your head in all situations, endure hardship, do the work of an evangelist, discharge all the duties of your ministry.

The writer to the Hebrews connects hardships, at times, to the discipline of God. Since hardships pushes us into reflective living, may we also reflect on what the Lord might want to teach us through the hardships we face.

> Hebrews 12:7-8 (NIV) 7 Endure hardship as discipline; God is treating you as his children. For what children are not disciplined by their father? 8 If you are not disciplined—and everyone undergoes discipline—then you are not legitimate, not true sons and daughters at all.

Facing hardships is not always the result of us being under God's discipline, it might also come when we in earnest pursue the vision God gave us, such as was the case with Nehemiah. He was a godly man with a heart to see the walls of Jerusalem rebuilt and restored. It was during this pursuit of the vision God placed in his heart that he encountered unparalleled hardship.

> Nehemiah 9:32 (NIV) "32 "Now therefore, our God, the great God, mighty and awesome, who keeps his covenant of love, do not let all this hardship seem trifling in your eyes—the hardship that has come on us, on our kings and leaders, on our priests and prophets, on our ancestors and all your people, from the days of the kings of Assyria until today.

Another example of hardship comes from Genesis 31 when Jacob recounts the hardships he endured under Laban. His hardship came from mistreatment, unfair working circumstances, sleepless nights, hunger, cold, the heat of day, and many more. When he finally left, God gave him a rich reward for all the hardships and ill-treatment he endured from his Father-in-law.

> Genesis 31:42 (NIV) "42 If the God of my father, the God of Abraham and the Fear of Isaac, had not been with me, you would surely have sent me away empty-handed. But God has seen my hardship and the toil of my hands, and last night he rebuked you."

I pray that when you face hardships in ministry that the hardships that these men of God endured will serve as encouragement for you to endure.

8. Hunger, starvation and famine.

Some of the hardships we might face can be compared with those that the Apostle Paul faced. In his letter to the Church in Corinth Paul mentioned some of the hardships he endured for the sake of the advancement of the Gospel.

> 2 Corinthians 6:3-10 (NIV) We put no stumbling block in anyone's path, so that our ministry will not be discredited. 4 Rather, as servants of God we commend ourselves in every way: in great endurance; in troubles, hardships and distresses; 5 in beatings, imprisonments and riots; in hard work, sleepless nights and hunger; 6 in purity, understanding, patience and kindness; in the Holy Spirit and in sincere love; 7 in truthful speech and in the power of God; with weapons of righteousness in the right hand and in the left; 8 through glory and dishonor, bad

> report and good report; genuine, yet regarded as impostors; 9 known, yet regarded as unknown; dying, and yet we live on; beaten, and yet not killed; 10 sorrowful, yet always rejoicing; poor, yet making many rich; having nothing, and yet possessing everything.

Many of us share this same report as if it was ours. My encouragement to you today is, endure. Stand strong in your faith and the calling with which God called you.

9. Spiritual and demonic attacks.

Sometimes we experience spiritual opposition in our work. These could be observed in the natural, but sometimes we are not able to discern exactly where the problem is. The Apostle Paul wrote about this spiritual dimension on a number of occasions.

> Ephesians 6:12-13 (NIV) 12 For our struggle is not against flesh and blood, but against the rulers, against the authorities, against the powers of this dark world and against the spiritual forces of evil in the heavenly realms. 13 Therefore put on the full armor of God, so that when the day of evil comes, you may be able to stand your ground, and after you have done everything, to stand.

This spiritual warfare cannot be fought by natural means. The only way to win this spiritual battle is by putting on the whole armour of God and by using the spiritual weapons of prayer, obedience and declaration.

> 2 Corinthians 10:3-4 (NIV) 3 For though we live in the world, we do not wage war as the world does. 4 The weapons we fight with are not the weapons of the world. On the contrary, they have divine power to

demolish strongholds.

When you have a sense that you're not succeeding and you can honestly not lay your finger on what the cause might be, remember that our wrestle is not against flesh or blood, but against the rulers, the principalities, the spiritual forces of darkness in the air.

This might not always be the enemy either who causes us to find ourselves up against a brick wall, sometimes it could be the Lord Himself. May I remind you of Balaam when he was contracted by a hostile King to curse Israel. It was the Lord who sent His Angel to block Balaam on his path.

In the New Testament we find the Apostles Paul and Barnabas on their first Missionary journey in Acts chapter 16.

> Acts 16:6-7 (NIV) 6 Paul and his companions travelled throughout the region of Phrygia and Galatia, having been kept by the Holy Spirit from preaching the word in the province of Asia. 7 When they came to the border of Mysia, they tried to enter Bithynia, but the Spirit of Jesus would not allow them to.

On both of these occasions it was the Holy Spirit who kept them from preaching the Word in those regions. The Holy Spirit spiritually challenged them to not preach the Word in those regions at that time. We need to be spiritually discerning as to the source of our spiritual opposition. Of course, we face spiritual challenges, and mostly from our great Adversary – Satan.

Paul stepped out to preach the Gospel in the region of Paphos to a certain proconsul, Sergius Paulus. It was here that Paul encountered a spiritual challenge in the person of Elymas the sorcerer who opposed them (v.8) and tried to turn the proconsul from believing. Now this is spiritual warfare. Paul was full of the Holy Spirit (v.9) and dealt decisively with this evil man. We too should always keep ourselves "full of the Holy Spirit" so that we will be able to deal in the same way with those opposing spiritual attacks.

> Acts 13:6-11 (NIV) 6 They traveled through the whole
> island until they came to Paphos. There they met a
> Jewish sorcerer and false prophet named Bar-Jesus, 7
> who was an attendant of the proconsul, Sergius
> Paulus. The proconsul, an intelligent man, sent for
> Barnabas and Saul because he wanted to hear the
> word of God. 8 But Elymas the sorcerer (for that is
> what his name means) opposed them and tried to
> turn the proconsul from the faith. 9 Then Saul, who
> was also called Paul, filled with the Holy Spirit,
> looked straight at Elymas and said, 10 "You are a
> child of the devil and an enemy of everything that is
> right! You are full of all kinds of deceit and trickery.
> Will you never stop perverting the right ways of the
> Lord? 11 Now the hand of the Lord is against you.
> You are going to be blind for a time, not even able to
> see the light of the sun." Immediately mist and
> darkness came over him, and he groped about,
> seeking someone to lead him by the hand.

This might be an extreme example; however, this is most certainly one of the challenges we might face in our pursuits of sharing the Gospel of Jesus Christ.

10. Physical and emotional challenges.

Our challenges are not always spiritual. Sometimes it is very much physical. A few years ago, a certain Mafia Leader made numerous attempts to bring harm to our growing church and since I did not give way to his manipulation and intimidation, he ensued more direct physical assaults. On a few occasions he came to my office with his bodyguard and got him to physically assault me to use this as a means to persuade me to give in to his demands. This was one of the most demanding times of my ministry.

I always remind myself that I am not the first to endure this kind of hostile treatment from people who oppose the advancement of the Gospel, and most certainly won't be the last. The Apostles endured such physical assaults many times.

> 2 Corinthians 6:3-5, 9 (NIV) We put no stumbling block in anyone's path, so that our ministry will not be discredited. 4 Rather, as servants of God we commend ourselves in every way: in great endurance; in troubles, hardships and distresses; 5 in beatings, imprisonments and riots; in hard work, sleepless nights and hunger; 9 known, yet regarded as unknown; dying, and yet we live on; beaten, and yet not killed;"

In reading some biographies of some great Missionaries I learnt of a number of them left their missionary assignments due to depression. We should always assess our mental wellbeing as we pursue the work set before us. There are a few things that most certainly helped me keep some kind of sanity when things did not make sense, and reading these biographies most certainly helped and encouraged me greatly.

I frequently travel to some countries where they still persecute preachers, and once I listen to their stories, I thank God for these faithful servants who advance the work of God despite being troubled, beaten, imprisoned, and facing hardships. May you too be encouraged that this has been the practice throughout history. May the Lord strengthen you to endure!

11. Evil speaking.

In preparing His Disciples, Jesus forewarned His Disciples that people would speak evil of them.

Matthew gives us an account of this forewarning.

> Matthew 5:10-12 (NIV) "10 Blessed are those who are persecuted because of righteousness, for theirs is the

kingdom of heaven. 11 "Blessed are you when people insult you, persecute you and falsely say all kinds of evil against you because of me. 12 Rejoice and be glad, because great is your reward in heaven, for in the same way they persecuted the prophets who were before you."

Jesus endured this kind of treatment from the religious leaders of his day. The Apostles Peter and Paul endured this kind of treatment many times as they continued to share the Word of God.

Mark 15:29-32 (NIV) 29 Those who passed by hurled insults at him, shaking their heads and saying, "So! You who are going to destroy the temple and build it in three days, 30 come down from the cross and save yourself!" 31 In the same way the chief priests and the teachers of the law mocked him among themselves. "He saved others," they said, "but he can't save himself! 32 Let this Messiah, this king of Israel, come down now from the cross, that we may see and believe. "Those crucified with him also heaped insults on him."

1 Peter 2:21,23 (NIV)"21To this you were called, because Christ suffered for you, leaving you an example, that you should follow in his steps. 23 When they hurled their insults at him, he did not retaliate; when he suffered, he made no threats. Instead, he entrusted himself to him who judges justly."

In both his letters to the Church in Corinth Paul wrote about his persecutions and the things he endures to advance the Gospel.

2 Corinthians 4:11-13 (NIV) 11 To this very hour we go hungry and thirsty, we are in rags, we are brutally

> treated, we are homeless. 12 We work hard with our own hands. When we are cursed, we bless; when we are persecuted, we endure it; 13 when we are slandered, we answer kindly. We have become the scum of the earth, the garbage of the world—right up to this moment.

In ministry you will endure this kind of treatment as well. Brace and prepare yourself that when it happens that you are not taken by surprise as if something strange has happened to you. I pray that you will learn during these challenging times to lean into God as your Protector, Guide and Shield. May the example of our Lord and that of the Apostle Paul serve as guidance and encouragement in how to deal with such personal and abusive assaults.

12. Transitioning and waiting challenges.

Sometimes we don't have the full picture revealed to us and a simple wait from the Lord has to suffice. ***How many times don't we receive that Word from the Lord, to wait?***

> Psalms 27:14 (NKJV) "14 Wait on the Lord; Be of good courage, And He shall strengthen your heart; Wait, I say, on the Lord!"

> Isaiah 40:31 (NKJV) "31 But those who wait on the Lord Shall renew their strength; They shall mount up with wings like eagles, They shall run and not be weary, They shall walk and not faint."

A time of waiting could be for our development and maturing in preparation for what God has in store for us. It might also be that the place where God wants us to go is not yet ready for our arrival. God is never late. He is always on time. He is not slow in answering. He is simply patient with us.

> Isaiah 64:4 (NIV) "4 Since ancient times no one has heard,
> no ear has perceived, no eye has seen any God
> besides you, who acts on behalf of those who wait
> for him.

Never make decisions in haste or when the answers don't seem to be at a time as you expect. Remember that God always has our best interest at heart. Whenever He makes us wait, He clearly has our welfare at heart. Be patient and wait for the Lord.

> Acts 1:4 (NIV) "4 On one occasion, while he was eating
> with them, he gave them this command: "Do not
> leave Jerusalem, but wait for the gift my Father
> promised, which you have heard me speak about."

One time Israel became insolent about entering into the Promised Land and simply wanted to go in on their own, but it was Moses' wisdom that prevailed with: "Unless the Lord Himself goes up with us, we don't go." Never leave the place where you are now until the Lord tells you to move and when He goes out with you. The advice in Lamentations serves as strong guidance to us to wait on the Lord before we do anything.

> Lamentations 3:25-26 (AMPC) "25The Lord is good to
> those who wait hopefully and expectantly for Him, to
> those who seek Him [inquire of and for Him and
> require Him by right of necessity and on the authority
> of God's word]. 26 It is good that one should hope in
> and wait quietly for the salvation (the safety and ease)
> of the Lord."

There are many blessings that God desires to bring to us as His Servants, so I encourage you to wait for His Guidance, Directives and empowerment. It was definitely worth the wait for the Disciples, when Jesus asked them to wait in Jerusalem for the Promise of the Father. Those 10 days made the difference between a global impacting ministry and not going anywhere. May you be encouraged to wait, every time when God says, "Wait" that you will patiently wait on Him.

13. Family and relational challenges.

One of the areas where I see that the enemy severely attack the Servants of God is the area of attacking their family and marriage relationships. Satan will use whatever avenue he can find to challenge your obedience and consistency in fulfilling the Call of God. In Jesus' teaching of His Disciples, He advised them that they needed to prepare themselves to even leave their family to fulfill the Call and Purpose of God.

> Matthew 19:27-30 (NIV) 27 Peter answered him, "We have left everything to follow you! What then will there be for us?" 28 Jesus said to them, "Truly I tell you, at the renewal of all things, when the Son of Man sits on his glorious throne, you who have followed me will also sit on twelve thrones, judging the twelve tribes of Israel. 29 And everyone who has left houses or brothers or sisters or father or mother or wife or children or fields for my sake will receive a hundred times as much and will inherit eternal life. 30 But many who are first will be last, and many who are last will be first.

Abraham's wife, Sarah, laughed at him and the faith He held on to that God would give him a son. David's wife, Michal, despised him for his great rejoicing as the Ark of God was brought back into Jerusalem.

> 2 Samuel 6:16 (NIV) "16 As the ark of the Lord was entering the City of David, Michal daughter of Saul watched from a window. And when she saw King David leaping and dancing before the Lord, she despised him in her heart."

Job faced many challenges, but surely one of the greatest was that his own wife would challenge him to "curse God and die." The closest companion of Job was his wife. She is the one who would stand with her husband through everything, but when she challenges him, he makes a choice to maintain his integrity. This must have been so hard. I have heard of many Great Men of God whose spouses left them since the challenges they faced were simply too much for them.

> Job 2:9-10 (NIV) "9 His wife said to him, "Are you still maintaining your integrity? Curse God and die!" 10 He replied, "You are talking like a foolish woman. Shall we accept good from God, and not trouble?" In all this, Job did not sin in what he said."

I don't know the challenges that you might face with your spouse or family, but all I can pray is that God would protect you and keep you and your family safe.

14. Financial challenges.

Another area where Pastors and Church Planters face challenges is with their finances. I daily receive requests for financial assistance, or for prayer regarding financial struggles, from Church Leaders around the world. Everywhere I go to speak on Church Planting I find that the interchangeable top requests for assistance I receive is that for Understanding Discipleship and for financial assistance. Strangely this is hardly expressed as being such a huge challenge by those Leaders in the Bible. Apart of the Apostle Paul mentioning his hardships of enduring "Hunger and Thirst" and "going without food," there is very little emphasis given to the financial struggles the Servants of God faced throughout history.

We live in a different age, and whereas their struggles might have been more on staying alive in the midst of severe persecutions and hostile treatment, and therefore their own welfare was of less importance than what we experience today. Most places where the church is growing and advancing nowadays has some kind of protection systems to secure their safety, and therefore the next area that then demands their care and concern is their physical welfare. The Apostle Paul mentioned the things he endured, and one of them was hunger.

> 2 Corinthians 6:4-5 (NIV) "4 Rather, as servants of God we commend ourselves in every way: in great endurance; in troubles, hardships and distresses; 5 in beatings, imprisonments and riots; in hard work, sleepless nights and hunger;"

> 2 Corinthians 11:27 (NIV) "27 I have labored and toiled and have often gone without sleep; I have known hunger and thirst and have often gone without food; I have been cold and naked."

His resolve was to learn to be content in whatever circumstances he lived. Through the years we faced many uncertain times. Most churches I know are solely dependent on the weekly offering and tithes of their members or coherent to support their Pastoral Staff. The average church size, around the world is about 85 people per congregation, and therefore the financial stability is highly susceptible to the coming and goings of those who attend and support the work. When an industry closes which impacts on a number of congregants losing their jobs, or if an internal feud between some members causes some families to leave, these have devastating effects on the local Church, but more so on the welfare of the Pastor and staff.

In the early years of my ministry, we lived from hand to mouth many months. Many months we never received a salary and had to survive on the alms and generosity of some who took pity on us, or at least that is how it felt. I know that this is how many of you, reading this book, feel, or even felt. The Apostle Paul helped me deal with this constant tension of living in the ups and downs of Sunday incomes. He said that the resolution is to learn to be content in whatever circumstance you find yourself in.

> Philippians 4:11-12 (NIV) 1 I am not saying this because I am in need, for I have learned to be content whatever the circumstances. 12 I know what it is to be in need, and I know what it is to have plenty. I have learned the secret of being content in any and every situation, whether well fed or hungry, whether living in plenty or in want.

Another thing that helped me succeed and endure through financial difficulties was learning to make the Lord my source and to take personal responsibility for the welfare of my family.

> 1 Timothy 3:5 (NIV) "5 (If anyone does not know how to manage his own family, how can he take care of God's church?)"

This meant that at times I had to become a bi-vocational pastor. I took on part-time work to take care of my family's needs. It is not the church's responsibility to take care of you and your family. It is your and my responsibility. Unless we take responsibility for our families, how can we take care of God's Church? The Apostle Paul worked as a tentmaker on a number of occasions to provide for his own personal needs. I do however believe that if you follow the strategy that I outlined in this book, that you will soon become a Servant of God who will live off the fruit of your labour in a full-time capacity.

15. Vision and Focus challenges.

Mother Theresa apparently once said: "It is a sad sight when people have eyes to see and have no vision." The Bible teaches this principle in a few places.

> Proverbs 29:18 (KJV) "18 Where there is no vision, the people perish: but he that keepeth the law, happy is he."

Most of what we read about in the Bible came as a result of receiving a vision or dream from the Lord. For Noah it was the design and life purpose of building an Ark. For Abraham it was the vision of having a son and taking possession of a foreign country. For Moses it was that Vision in the desert that propelled him into his destiny. David lived by the frequent visions and dreams he received from God. For the prophets of old, or "Seers" as they were often termed and referred to, they wrote these messages down from visions they had.

In ministry it is so vitally important that we always live within the parameters of the visions and dreams we received from God. Fulfilling the assignments, we receive through visions is what ministry is all about. If you've become uncertain about what you're supposed to be doing, then it's time for you to take a prayer and fasting retreat to go and seek the Lord for a fresh vision. A vision is a God-given vision, dream or instruction you receive through prayer that clearly assigns you to work to a determined goal or purpose.

16. Authority challenges.

Another challenge we face in ministry is that of our Authority being challenged. Your position and your anointing will be challenged. People will question your Calling, your Authority and the decisions you make. This first happened to Joseph, when he shared the dreams God gave him, with his Brothers and Parents. They immediately questioned him envisioning having authority over them. They hated him, because they possibly knew that God revealed His plan for Joseph's life, and they were not pleased about God's Choice. In most instances it is exactly that same spirit that is in operation. People don't like the choice God made of who should have authority and rule over them.

> Genesis 37:8 (NIV) "8 His brothers said to him, "Do you intend to reign over us? Will you actually rule us?" And they hated him all the more because of his dream and what he had said."

The same thing happened to Moses when he led the Israelites out of Egypt to the promised land. Right from when Moses realised God's purpose for his life, his authority was questioned.

> Exodus 2:14 (NIV) "14 The man said, "Who made you ruler and judge over us? Are you thinking of killing me as you killed the Egyptian?" Then Moses was afraid and thought, "What I did must have become known.""

During their trek through the wilderness enroute to the Promised land, a few leaders rebelled against Moses and against Aaron. When Moses summoned them to come, they refused. Their refusal was a clear sign of their rebellion against the Authority God placed over them.

> Numbers 16:12-14 (NIV) 12 Then Moses summoned Dathan and Abiram, the sons of Eliab. But they said, "We will not come! 13 Isn't it enough that you have brought us up out of a land flowing with milk and honey to kill us in the wilderness? And now you also want to lord it over us! 14 Moreover, you haven't brought us into a land flowing with milk and honey or given us an inheritance of fields and vineyards. Do you want to treat these men like slaves? No, we will not come!"

We know that God dealt with these rebellious people, and their families in a decisive way and opened the earth and swallowed them up. This should be a lesson to all, however, sadly, few people, especially nowadays, give any respect to those whom God called and anointed for Holy Service. If it happened to Moses and Aaron, it would happen to you, they will question your authority. As long as what you continue in making Holy Spirit inspired decisions and earnestly pursue the guidance and directives of the Holy Spirit on a daily basis, you should be fine. You too will endure through faith, prayer and perseverance.

The last Judge that ruled Israel was the Prophet Samuel. He was a true man of God! However, when the spirit of the world got hold of the people, they insisted that they wanted a King just like the other nations. Samuel felt strong rejection, but even after pleading with the people and with God, God directed him to appoint a king as per their request.

> 1 Samuel 8:6-7 (NIV) 6 But when they said, "Give us a king to lead us," this displeased Samuel; so he prayed to the Lord. 7 And the Lord told him: "Listen to all that the people are saying to you; it is not you they have rejected, but they have rejected me as their king."

> 1 Samuel 8:19-22 (NIV) 19 But the people refused to listen to Samuel. "No!" they said. "We want a king over us. 20 Then we will be like all the other nations, with a king to lead us and to go out before us and fight our battles." 21 When Samuel heard all that the people said, he repeated it before the Lord. 22 The Lord answered, "Listen to them and give them a king."

It is a sad day when God tell us to do what the people want. That day brings famine, destitution and sorrow. In ministry, our only resolve when people continue in their persistence to not listen to the Word of the Lord, is for us to pray and do what God would have us do. Sometimes it will feel as if you're the only person on the planet who is still holding on to principles of the Word of God, stand strong, hold fast onto your faith and pray. Prayer solidifies our faith but also brings much needed guidance when our authority and leading is questioned.

Even Jesus' authority was questioned by the high priest, a religious leader of His day.

> Mark 11:27-28 (NIV) "27 They arrived again in Jerusalem, and while Jesus was walking in the temple courts, the chief priests, the teachers of the law and the elders came to him. 28 "By what authority are you doing these things?" they asked. "And who gave you authority to do this?""

Just in case you've become confused and unsure: God placed anointing and authority on each one of His Called Servants. You are anointed for a purpose and God anoints you with authority.

> Hebrews 13:17 (NIV) "17 Have confidence in your leaders and submit to their authority, because they keep watch over you as those who must give an account. Do this so that their work will be a joy, not a burden, for that would be of no benefit to you."

Finally, may I remind you that one of the only three elements that God instructed to be kept in the Ark of the Covenant is the budded rod of Aaron, an eternal reminder of God's choosing and appointment from among men.

> Hebrews 9:3-5 (KJV) "3 And after the second veil, the tabernacle which is called the Holiest of all; 4 Which had the golden censer, and the ark of the covenant overlaid roundabout with gold, wherein was the golden pot that had manna, and Aaron's rod that budded, and the tables of the covenant; 5 And over it the Cherubims of glory shadowing the Mercyseat; of which we cannot now speak particularly."

It is never a pleasant experience when people challenge your authority. I pray that these few references, among many, will serve as an encouragement for you when you face this challenge.

HOW DO WE PREPARE OURSELVES TO MEET THESE CHALLENGES?

I learned a few lessons about the sacrifices we might have to make as we go through the challenges. I pray that these brief observations might be helpful to you as well. The first is a lesson that I learned from a couple of articles on men and woman who succeeded in doing extra-ordinary things in their lives is that of being mentally and spiritually prepared.

1. Be Mentally and Spiritually prepared.

The story of Sir Edmund Hillary, and his incredible mountaineering success, by becoming the first person to summit Mount Everest in Nepal in 1953, taught us incredible lessons on succeeding through the most extreme and strenuous circumstances. One of the key aspects of his incredible success is that he prepared himself spiritually and mentally. We will do ourselves a great favour if we too will prepare ourselves beforehand that we will encounter and experience these kinds of hostilities against us and our ministry.

The writer of the Book to the Hebrews, in chapter 11, records the names of those who paid a high price for the advancement of the message of Hope. It seems from the Bible that they encouraged each other by that which was known so that they would endure the harness of the challenges they faced.

2. It might cost you your business, job or vocation.

One of the essential preparations we need to embrace ourselves with before we embark on our pursuit of planting Dynamic Churches is that it will come at a price, a high price, and at most it might cost you everything you have. This was true for the Apostles and it will be true for us.

Matthew 4:18-22 (NIV) " [18] As Jesus was walking beside

> the Sea of Galilee, he saw two brothers, Simon called Peter and his brother Andrew. They were casting a net into the lake, for they were fishermen. [19] "Come, follow me," Jesus said, "and I will make you fishers of men." [20] At once they left their nets and followed him. [21] Going on from there, he saw two other brothers, James son of Zebedee and his brother John. They were in a boat with their father Zebedee, preparing their nets. Jesus called them, [22] and immediately they left the boat and their father and followed him."

These Disciples left their boats, their businesses and vocations to follow the Call of Jesus. It might cost you your business, vocation and possessions. This is most certainly what it cost the Disciples as they followed the Lord Jesus.

When Jesus encountered the rich young man, He challenged him to sell all his possessions.

> Matthew 19:21 (NIV) "21 Jesus answered, 'If you want to be perfect, go, sell your possessions and give to the poor, and you will have treasure in heaven. Then come, follow me.'"

When Christ taught His Disciples of the cost of being His follower, He went on to tell them the full extent of what this might mean. In His answer to Peter's plea that they already "left everything," Jesus actually encouraged him with the "reward" that awaits those who "left" everything for Him.

> Matthew 19:27-29 (NIV) "27 Peter answered him, "We have left everything to follow you! What then will there be for us?" 28 Jesus said to them, "Truly I tell you, at the renewal of all things, when the Son of Man sits on his glorious throne, you who have followed me will also sit on twelve thrones, judging the twelve tribes of Israel. 29 And everyone who has left houses

or brothers or sisters or father or mother or wife or children or fields for my sake will receive a hundred times as much and will inherit eternal life."

3. It will cost you to deny yourself often.

Mark 8:34-38 (KJV) "[34] And when he had called the people unto him with his disciples also, he said unto them, Whosoever will come after me, let him deny himself, and take up his cross, and follow me."

10

HOW TO SUCCEED IN CHURCH PLANTING

I believe God desire to give us success in our ministries. Success is never guaranteed, however, the following commitments on our part will most certainly increase our chances of succeeding.

A research study on the achievement and paralleled preparation of elite Olympic athletes highlighted a number of areas on which they concentrated which, in turn, added to their ultimate success According to Orlick (2000), there are seven critical elements of excellence that guide the pursuit of performance excellence on a consistent basis: commitment, focus, confidence, positive images, mental readiness, distraction control, and ongoing learning.

1. It will take a Full Commitment.

Church Planting requires a full commitment. We cannot pursue Church Planting with a Hireling attitude or commitment. To succeed, you will have to lay down your life for the sheep. It is not a job, where you just work for a wage and once you don't receive a wage, then you look for another job that can pay you a wage. In the words of Jesus, you need the commitment of being a Shepherd.

John 10:11-13 (NIV) "[11] "I am the good shepherd. The good shepherd lays down his life for the sheep. The hired hand is not the shepherd who owns the sheep. So when he sees the wolf coming, he abandons the sheep and runs away. Then the wolf attacks the flock and scatters it. [13] The man runs away because he is a hired hand and cares nothing for the sheep."

Make a commitment before you enter that you will stand, regardless.

2. It will require Focus.

As Church Planters we need to be focused and engaged. As important as vision is to keep us from perishing, focus is to keep us engaged to see those visions fulfilled.

3. It will require Confidence.

Confidence is the feeling you have that you can trust and rely on someone or something. As a Church Planter you need confidence in God, the vision He has given you, His anointing upon your life and that of your team. Confidence in yourself, your abilities and skills are essential to successful church planting. The writer to the Hebrews tells us that we should not throw away our confidence since it will be richly rewarded if we persevere and continue to complete what God assigned for us to do.

Hebrews 10:35-36 (NIV) "[35] So do not throw away your confidence; it will be richly rewarded. [36] You need to persevere so that when you have done the will of God, you will receive what he has promised.

Ephesians 3:12 (KJV) "[12] In whom we have boldness and access with confidence by the faith of him.

4. You need to develop and keep Positive images.

Since there are so many things that we encounter in Church Planting that might try to distort our image of God, His Church and His Purpose. Keep your eyes on the Lord Jesus. Keep reminding yourself of the Good things God has done.

> Colossians 3:2 (AMPC) "2 And set your minds and keep them set on what is above (the higher things), not on the things that are on the earth.

> Hebrews 12:2 (NIV 1984) 2 Let us fix our eyes on Jesus, the author and perfecter of our faith, who for the joy set before him endured the cross, scorning its shame, and sat down at the right hand of the throne of God.

By Keeping our eyes focused on Jesus, and all that He has done for us, along with a grateful heart, it will both keep us protected, and help us keep positive images and visions alive in our hearts.

5. You need to have Mental readiness.

Most of our preparedness happens in our minds. Joyce Meyer speaks of "The Battlefield of the Mind." As applicable as what it is for athletes to be mentally prepared during their solitary times of practice and exercise, and when they get on the track to race, it is important for us to constantly keep our minds actively prepared for action, either in our times of devotion or when we step out in the world.

> 1 Peter 1:13 (NIV 1984) "13 Therefore, prepare your minds for action; be self-controlled; set your hope fully on the grace to be given you when Jesus Christ is revealed.

> Luke 21:14 (AMPC) "14 Resolve and settle it in your minds not to meditate and prepare beforehand how

you are to make your defense and how you will answer.

6. You will need Distraction control.

Many Church Planters struggle with distraction control. We get distracted by unnecessary things like doing things others could do. It might be doing the banking, or taking out post, mowing the lawn or cleaning the Place of Worship. Don't let menial tasks keep you from doing what God Called and Anointed you for.

What we learn from Jesus and His Disciples was their ability to keep focused and not to be distracted by task, that might have importance, but not being primary to what God wants us to do. For the Apostles they practiced "Distraction Control" when there arose a feud among the widows, they determined that it was more expedient to continue on prayer and preaching than to serve the table. This is a great example of one area where many Pastors get distracted.

> Acts 6:2-4 (NIV) "2 So the Twelve gathered all the disciples together and said, "It would not be right for us to neglect the ministry of the word of God in order to wait on tables. 3 Brothers and sisters, choose seven men from among you who are known to be full of the Spirit and wisdom. We will turn this responsibility over to them 4 and will give our attention to prayer and the ministry of the word."

7. You need to make a commitment to Ongoing learning.

There is a saying: *"**Leaders are Readers.**"* One of the characteristics of successful Leaders is their ability to always remain teachable and to be open to learn new things. Study is good. I pray that you too will embrace the advice Paul gave his spiritual son, Timothy, to study. I read a lot and I learn a lot. Even though I had the privilege of equipping Church Planters and Leaders in over 70 nations (by 2017) I still learn new things and ways in which we can advance the cause of Church Planting.

> 2 Timothy 2:15 (AMPC) "15 Study and be eager and do your utmost to present yourself to God approved (tested by trial), a workman who has no cause to be ashamed, correctly analyzing and accurately dividing [rightly handling and skillfully teaching] the Word of Truth."

8. It will require absolute Obedience.

Obedience is an essential characteristic and value in the Kingdom of God. Our obedience to God, His Will as defined to us through His Word, and to those whom He placed over us, will most certainly increase our chances for success. Many Church Planters are great at being focused and intentional in execution of their assignment, however, come undone when they remain stubborn and closed to receive wise counsel from those who have gone before them. As mentioned earlier, a Discipler, a Pastor, a Counsellor, to whom we submit for guidance and sound advice will only serve their God-given role when we submit to, and obey, their advice, instruction and directives.

> 1 John 2:3 (NIV) "3 We know that we have come to know him if we obey his commands.

It stems from our heartfelt obedience to the Lordship of Christ in our lives. May we fully obey the Lord, in everything He asks or demands of us. Finally, God is a Rewarder, and if nothing else motivates you or keeps you focused and enduring, then let the Holy Spirit remind you of the Reward of the Lord.

9. Our Reward is with the Lord.

The Word of God, repeatedly, tells us of the Reward of God. This Reward is held for those who persevere and succeed.

> Hebrews 11:6 (NIV) "6 And without faith it is impossible to please God, because anyone who comes to him must believe that he exists and that he rewards those who earnestly seek him.

> Revelation 22:12 (NIV 1984) "12 "Behold, I am coming soon! My reward is with me, and I will give to everyone according to what he has done."

> Colossians 3:23-24 (NIV 1984) "23 Whatever you do, work at it with all your heart, as working for the Lord, not for men, 24 since you know that you will receive an inheritance from the Lord as a reward. It is the Lord Christ you are serving.

I pray that you will be counted among those who endured, persevered and succeeded.

11

SIMPLE HOUSE CHURCH PLANTING

In conclusion of this short training, may I encourage you to start where you are right now. Start in your house! If you sense the Call of God upon your life, then start with yourself and then with those in your house, and then with those in your sphere of influence.

The early church started in a house. The house is the place where our values are measured and scrutinised more than anywhere else. I pray that your life in Christ would experience such a transformation that those close to you will see and recognize the impact of the Holy Spirit's work in you.

Many Pastors tell me that they have a dream of seeing an Acts Church planted where people will be added to the Church on a daily basis and where signs and wonders will be in the order of every day. Well, it is possible when we apply ourselves with the same diligence to the teachings of the Lord Jesus and His Apostles and apply the same spiritual disciplines and Kingdom values in our lives.

I have jotted down a few simple guidelines as a reminder of our time together, as well as a quick guide or overview as to the task before you:

Step 1. Before you start

1. Count the cost

During our last session we looked at the "Cost of Church Planting." I pray that you will take the time to consider the path that lies before you. Even though I, and many others know what lies before us, we would still do what we do now because we are "dead men working." Christ set us this example.

2. Affiffirm God's Call to plant this Cell Church

Before you even start dreaming about possibilities, make sure that you have been Called by God to be a Church Planter. All of us have been called to advance the Kingdom of God as part of the Body of Christ, however, only some have been Called to lead the planting of a Dynamic Church. You definitely need that Call and Grace of God on your life. Be sure to affirm the Call of God, as explored in the Chapter on "the Call to Church Planting" session.

3. Ensure the Elementary Foundations are laid, and Spiritual Disciplines established

Hebrews 6 verses 1-2 points us to six Elementary Foundations to establish in our faith. Through Jesus' Teachings on the Mountain and throughout the Gospels, we learned that the Kingdom of God has Values and demands Spiritual Disciplines to keep those Values in place in our lives.

a. Values of the Kingdom of God.

Matthew 5 from verse 3 shares with us the Values of the Kingdom of God. Nothing impacts people more than a Transformed life. Embracing and living the Values impacts people much more than words, without a demonstration of a changed life. Learn the Values as Jesus taught them and apply them in willing obedience.

b. Spiritual Disciplines

Jesus taught His Disciples Spiritual Disciplines; "When you pray," "When you fast," "When you give." There are many spiritual disciplines to explore and assimilate into our daily lives. The Spiritual Disciplines of Fasting and Prayer, Stewardship, Simplicity, Servanthood, studying and meditating on the Word of God, are some of the most valued disciplines to uphold. You can read more on these in my Book on "The Values and Spiritual Disciplines of the Kingdom of God." Spiritual disciplines will keep the fire of God burning ablaze inside of you.

4. Wait until you're empowered from on High.

We need the Power of the Holy Spirit in our lives. Do not proceed any further unless you had a dedicated time of Fasting and Prayer for the empowerment of the Holy Spirit upon your life.

Step 2. Steps to start:

a. Seek a Worthy Man of Peace.

- Look for a lost person who has a good reputation with outsiders.
- Look for owners of businesses, leaders in industry and professional people.
- Look for people who will follow you.

b. Seek and save lost people.

- Build relationships with people in the Church.
- Build relationships with those outside the Church.
- Build relationships for a purpose.

c. Baptize those who accept Jesus as Lord and make a firm commitment to Christ.

d. Gather those whom you sense God has given you to start your first discipleship group.

Step 3. From individual ministry to discipleship group formation.

Up to this point your ministry centered on you and your personal development as a Disciple of Christ. It also focused on you reaching out to lost people, but specifically to "Worthy People" who will be your first Disciples and through whom you will lead the planting of a Dynamic Church.

1. Stage One – Group formation to take place at least weekly.

This is a Highly directive process where you Disciple the "Worthy men" God gave you. Meet weekly and teach them the following ***Elementary, Foundational Principles,*** Kingdom ***Values,*** Spiritual ***Disciplines,*** and ***Kingdom Identities***:

1. Foundational Principles of following Christ. Hebrews 6:1-2.
2. Kingdom Values. 52 Kingdom of God values and the Apostles Teachings.
3. Kingdom Identity:
4. Household of God,
5. Priesthood,
6. Bride of Christ,
7. Temple of the Holy Spirit.
8. Kingdom of God spiritual disciplines.
9. Minister through the Power of the Holy Spirit.

Each time you meet, prepare yourself to minister to them in the Power of the Holy Spirit. What you do at the beginning is what they will do at the beginning. Never be intimidated with numbers. "***Where***

two or three gathers together. The Church will only be as strong as what it is strong in groups of two or three. If the Church runs on all cylinders with "twos and three's" then it will run well when everyone congregates together. If you value each one, and each opportunity to minister, whether there be two or many, your disciples will place the same value on the opportunities and the people, God gives them. Remember, you are building Value and are developing DNA of the Church you dream to have and lead. Do so with patient endurance. Your efforts and diligence will soon be well rewarded.

1. Pray for them, each other, and for souls to be saved.
2. Establish them in Spiritual Disciplines so that they will get to know the voice of the Holy Spirit through prayer and the reading of the Word of God.
3. Teach them to obey everything Jesus taught us.

2. Stage Two – Teach them to Disciple others. (Balance being Directive and Facilitation.)

The second stage of in the phase of moving from individual ministry to group formation and discipleship is to equip your disciples to fulfil the purpose God has for them. Teach them that it will cost them everything, and that they are required to lay down their lives for the sake of Christ. Teach them about Stewardship; that everything we have, belongs to God, and we are mere Stewards entrusted with His possessions. We need to use it in a way that would bring glory and honour to Him. Teach them about "laying up treasures in Heaven" and honouring God with the "first fruits" of their labours. Teach them about sowing and reaping, and the giving to the poor. Teach them how to share their faith.

1. Counting the Cost of Discipleship.
2. Stewardship.
3. Witnessing.
4. Learning and Sharing. (Go make…)
5. Learning and Caring. (Compassion…)

6. Reporting and feedback. (Humility…)

3. Stage Three – Fruitfulness (High facilitation)

1. Disciples reach their first souls.
2. Disciples gather their first disciples in a group to start stage one.
3. Disciples take their disciples through stages.

4. Stage Four – Multiplication (Encouragement.)

1. Disciple's disciples reach their first souls.
2. Disciple's disciples gather their first disciples in a group to start stage one.
3. Disciple's Disciples take their disciples through stages.

Afterword

I pray that these brief outlines might assist you as you pursue the Call of God on your life. Godspeed.

Go, and make Disciples, Baptise them, and Teach them to obey everything Jesus taught us.

Let your light so shine before men that they will Glorify God!

OTHER BOOKS BY DR. HENDRIK J. VORSTER

Discipleship Foundations - Step One - Salvation Disciple Manual

Step One - Salvation

This Course explores the "How to" be Born Again and to establish a solid Foundation for your faith in Jesus Christ. It is based on Hebrews chapter 6 verses 1 and 2, and explores:

Repentance of dead works,
Faith in God,
Baptisms,
Laying on of hands,
Resurrection of the dead, and
Eternal Judgement

Teacher Manuals and Video Teaching material are available through our website:

www.churchplantinginstitute.com or at www.amazon.com

Discipleship Foundations Step Two - Values and Spiritual Disciplines Disciple Manual

Step Two - Values and Spiritual Disciplines Disciple Manual

This Course explores the "How to" develop spiritual disciplines as well as 52 Values Jesus taught. It is based on the teachings of Jesus to His Disciples, and explores:

Spiritual Disciplines

The disciplines we explore are: Reading, meditating on the Word of God, Prayer, Stewardship, Fasting, Servanthood, Simplicity, Worship, and Witnessing.

Values of the Kingdom of God

Humility, Mournfulness, meekness, Spiritual Passion, Mercifulness, Purity, Peacemaker, Patient endurance, Example, Custodian, Reconciliatory, Resoluteness, Loving, Discreetness, Forgiving, Kingdom of God Investor, God-minded, Kingdom of God prioritiser, Introspective, Persistent, Considerate, Conservative, Fruit-bearing, Practitioner, Accountability, Faithful, Childlikeness, Unity, Servanthood, Loyalty, Gratefulness, Stewardship, Obedience, Carefulness, Compassion, Caring, Confidence, Steadfastness, Contentment, Teachable, Deference, Diligence, Trustworthiness, Gentleness, Discernment, Truthfulness, Generous, Kindness, Watchfulness, Perseverance, Honouring and Submissive.

Teacher Manuals and Video Teaching material are available through our website:

www.churchplantinginstitute.com or at www.amazon.com

Discipleship Foundations Step Three - Developing Gifts and Skills

Step Three - Developing Gifts and Skills

This course is run through five weekend encounters. These weekend encounters have been designed to help Disciples discover their spiritual gifts, as well as learn skills to use their gifts, and to serve the Lord for the extension of His Kingdom. The Weekend Encounters are:

Gifts Discovery Weekend Encounter

We learn about Ministerial Office gifts, Service gifts, and Supernatural Spiritual Gifts. We discover our own, and then learn How we may use them to build up the local Church.

Survey of the Bible Weekend Encounter

During this weekend we do a survey of the Bible, from Genesis to Revelation. We also learn about the History of the Bible as well as How we can make most of our time in the Word.

Sharing your Faith Weekend Encounter

During this weekend we learn about the Gospel message, and How to share our faith effectively.

Overcoming Weekend Encounter

During this weekend we deal with those thistles and thorns that smother the growth and harvest of the good seed sown into our lives. We address How to overcome fear, unforgiveness, lust and the cares of the world with faith and obedience.

Shepherd Leader Weekend Encounter

During this weekend encounter we learn about being a Good Shepherd, and How to best disciple in a small group.

Teacher Manuals and Video Teaching material are available from our website:

www.churchplantinginstitute.com or at www.amazon.com

Discipleship Foundations Step Four - Fruitfulness

Step Four - Discipling Fruit-Producers

We were saved to serve. This course has been designed to mobilise Believers, from Learners to Practitioners. These sessions have been prepared for individual use, with those who are bearing fruit, and want to produce more fruit. Developing these areas in a sustained and systematic manner will ensure both fruitfulness and multiplication. Attending to these areas will ensure that you bear lasting fruit.

We explore:

1. Introduction.
2. Walking with purpose.
3. Build purposeful relationships. Finding Worthy Men
4. Priesthood. Praying effectively for those entrusted to you.
5. Caring compassionately.
6. Walking worthily.
7. Walking in the Spirit.
8. Practicing hospitality.

Teacher Manuals and Video Teaching material are available from our COURSES link from our website at:

www.churchplantinginstitute.com or at www.amazon.com

Discipleship Foundations Step Five - Multiplication

Step Five - Multiplication

This course was designed to assist fruit-producing disciples to live a life that will encourage a lifetime of fruitfulness. It will also give our disciples skills and guidelines to navigate their disciples through seasons of challenge and growth. This course is packed with Leadership advancing principles. The more these areas are addressed and encouraged, the more we will experience growth and multiplication. We explore:

1. Vision and dreams.
2. Set Godly Goals.
3. Character development
4. Gifts development - Impartation and Activation
5. Fruitfulness comes through constant challenge.
6. Relationships - Family, Children and Friends
7. The Power of encouragement
8. Finances - Personal and Ministry finances
9. Dealing with setbacks

- How to deal with failure?
- How to deal with betrayal?
- How to deal with rejection?
- How to deal with trials?
- How to deal with despondency?

10. Eternal rewards

Teacher Manuals and Video Teaching material are available from our website:

www.churchplantinginstitute.com or at www.amazon.com

Values
of the
Kingdom
of
God

Dr. Hendrik J. Vorster

Values of the Kingdom of God

By Dr. Hendrik J Vorster

Everyone desires to be known as a pleasant to be around with kind of person. This book helps you develop values towards such a godly character. This book explores 52 Values of the Kingdom of God.

Books are available from our website:

www.churchplantinginstitute.com or at www.amazon.com

SPIRITUAL
DISCIPLINES
OF THE
KINGDOM
OF
GOD

Spiritual Disciplines of the Kingdom of God

By Dr. Hendrik J Vorster

Every Believer desires to be a Fruit-producing branch in the Vineyard of our Lord. Developing spiritual disciplines is to develop spiritual roots from which our faith can draw sap to grow strong and fruit-bearing branches. This Book explores Nine Spiritual Disciplines of the Kingdom of God.

Books are available from our website:

www.churchplantinginstitute.com

Church Planting

How to plant a dynamic church

Dr. Hendrik J. Vorster

Foreword by: Dr. Yonggi Cho

Church Planting - by Dr Hendrik J Vorster

Church Planting - How to plant a dynamic, disciple-making church

By Dr Hendrik J Vorster

This is a handbook for those who wish to plant a disciple-making church. This book explores every aspect of church planting, and is widely used in over 70 Nations on 6 Continents. Here is a list of the areas that are explored:

1. The challenge to plant New Churches
2. Phases of Church Planting
3. Phase One of Church Planting - The Calling, Vision and Preparation Phase
4. The Call to Church Planting
5. Twelve Characteristics of Church Planting Leaders
6. Church Planting Terminology
7. Phase Two of Church Planting - Discipleship
8. The Process of Discipleship
9. Phase Three of Church Planting - Congregating the Discipleship Groups
10. Understanding Church Planting Finances
11. Understanding Church staff
12. Phase Four of Church Planting - Ministry development and Church Launching Phase
13. Understanding and Implementing Systems
14. Phase Five of Church Planting - Multiplication
15. Understanding the challenges in Church Planting
16. How to succeed in Church Planting
17. How to plant a House Church

Student Manuals and Video Teaching material are available from our website:

www.churchplantinginstitute.com or at www.amazon.com

www.ingramcontent.com/pod-product-compliance
Lightning Source LLC
LaVergne TN
LVHW010620100826
845148LV00014B/3040

* 9 7 8 1 7 3 6 6 4 2 6 8 9 *